HOW TO B

HOW TO B

Virginia Loo

SADDLE ROAD PRESS

Saddle Road Press
Ithaca, NY
saddleroadpress.com

Interior and cover design by Don Mitchell

ISBN 9798990054332
Library of Congress Control Number: 2024945944

For B
(but not until you are 18 and older)

CONTENTS

Cliff Jumping	9
What's the Plan?	17
Who's Your Daddy?	31
All Natural	39
Homemade Baby of Your Dreams	51
The Professionals	67
Chances Are	78
Kindness and Strangers	90
Give It Up	100
Hard to Say	110
Crazy Gods' Eyes	123
Choking	137
Tit Invaders	159
Passing	173
Containment	187
The Father the Son	198
Wasting	210
Spit It Out	223
If I Were You	235
Epilogue: Sublimation	242
Afterward	245
Acknowledgements	247
About the Author	248

CLIFF JUMPING

"I WANT A BABY."

The first time I said it out loud to anyone, I almost shouted it. I was standing on a small balcony about six stories up overlooking a large concrete deck. I might have been Eva Peron waving to her people below. Except I was in Rangoon, Burma, on a consultancy standing on a small balcony attached to a room of the old Shwedagon Pagoda Hotel. I was shouting over the loud and inefficient condenser of a split AC unit. Sharing the balcony with me and the condenser was my boss for the week, Oscar. The glass panes on the balcony door behind us were fogged up, my glasses had slipped down with the sweat on my nose. It was the first time I had been in Burma, but the humidity and the decay of the '60s-era buildings were familiar. Oscar needed a cigarette break, and by that time, three or four days into my mission, I was mildly addicted to his second-hand smoke.

I had arrived to conduct a workshop for Ministry of Health staff. And from the warren of WHO offices on the 7th floor of the Shwedagon, I had been doggedly preparing the materials for the workshop. The offices were reconfigured guest rooms—last remodeled sometime in the early '80s. Although the beds and TVs had been removed, each office still had its own personal bathroom. The bathtubs were filled with boxes of WHO publications, sometimes personal protective equipment, and operational supplies because a

WHO office always needs more storage. The hotel room "No Smoking" placards continued to be relevant and resented. Smoking breaks were commonplace.

How often in your life do you say, "I want a baby" out loud? How many people in your life can you say that to who are not the people (plural?) that you expect to make babies with? And under what circumstance would you ever be caught dead saying it out loud if you're a single woman in your thirties?

That day, when I said, "I want a baby," I had been declarative. I made the kind of statement you expect to be followed up by action. That day, I wasn't wistful. Not, "I want to have a baby one day," or "I always wanted to have a baby." Not my usual rueful statement, "if I want to have babies, I need to do it soon." That day, it came out of my mouth with the wild confidence of a cliff diver plunging to the parking deck below.

That day, I laid it out there. But saying "I want a baby" felt vulnerable. To let the people around you know what you want, while being uncertain about whether you will get it, opens you up to hurt. Someone with no tact might point out what is already obvious to you, that you're not in a relationship, that your clock is ticking, and it looks like it's not going to happen. Someone judge-y might say, "well you're not really serious because you're not putting all your effort into making 'it' happen." Another person might tell you not to worry about things you don't have control over, just accept your fate, but secretly tell others that the situation is really very sad. All of these people could be your mother. That's why it's best not to say things like "I want a baby" out loud.

Someone told me this was the place I should talk about why I wanted a baby. But sitting down to write it out, I drew a blank. Usually, the question to women is, why *don't* you want to have children. When I told people about my plan to have a baby, nobody ever said to me, "why do you want to do that?" People assume you have these strong primal yearnings to be a mother, what is there to explain? So when someone asks you to actually explain it, what is the right answer? The one that will satisfy the person asking? What do people want to hear?

I could say I always expected to have kids, as if its being a foregone conclusion implied that I always wanted kids. But that's deflection, just evading the question. I'd be disingenuous if I said I always liked kids. I never considered teaching and I never worked summers as a camp counselor or volunteered to be a youth leader, because I didn't find it enjoyable to spend a lot of time with kids. My mother is the same way. I don't think she likes kids, except her own. I've never heard her ask to hold someone else's baby. She doesn't like animals either, except her own emotionally-needy cats. I think that part is stranger than the fact that she has two kids. Her mother was the same, too, the part about not liking kids. What an ironic trait to inherit.

Then what is it that drove me to want to have a baby on my own? On paper, the motivation I attributed to myself sounds harsh: to have someone to take care of me when I'm old; to have someone to leave a legacy to; to fulfill a part of my female potential. Doesn't it sound pretty self-serving? But I suspect I wanted to have kids the way people in couples want to have kids. I hoped having kids would allow me to experience a certain kind of joy and pride and belonging. But pursuing this desire in the way I intended butted up against a bluff of dread. I wasn't sure if my having a baby counted as building a family—at least in the minds of some groups of people I know are out there. The kind of family I could create by myself could be described as an unwed mother and illegitimate child. Which seemed kind of *less than*. We would start off in the category of being an incomplete, if not broken, family. Who would say they want that?

Then how surprising that I said it so out loud and so confidently to someone like Oscar. We weren't strangers, but we had only passing social contact when I had been living in Delhi a few years before. There was one memorable dinner party, at a big compound with peacocks rustling in the Ashoka trees, a tasty French farmed chicken poached in a second hen's broth, and fifteen minutes of sudden pitch blackness due to an unplanned power cut. The night was cool and dark except for the warm glowing tips of people's cigarettes, shards of conversation, and the occasional crackling laughter of Oscar.

During this trip to Burma, we had figured out some other things we had in common. We both liked sweet, slightly tortured, frumpy white guys, and we loved binge watching episodes of *Frasier* and *Lost* on DVD. Another remarkable fact about Oscar that I discovered was that he was probably the only person in Asia whose DVD collection was completely legit. I was amazed to find out he owned all these non-pirated boxed sets. That he would spend real money for official copies of these shows, reflected his deeply principled, yet silly, soul.

When we first re-met in Rangoon and he heard me speak, Oscar blurted out, "You're so American!" And laughed in surprise because my face was so not. When traveling in Asia, I often passed for a local—in Thailand, the Philippines, sometimes in Nepal or the northeast of India, and always in Burma. Even when I explain I was American, people in Asia don't really quite believe it.

I grew up in Hawai'i, where being Asian is irrelevant to determining whether you're local. But having gone to college and working on the Continent, it's definitely not every place in the US that people consider me American, either. Oscar's reaction pleased me so much. I know he didn't just mean I had an American accent. His comment was more about my manner, how I talked, how my face expressed itself, my inclination toward congeniality, the optimism that comes with privilege. It so clearly identified me as "American." He saw me the way I saw myself.

Oscar told me that I reminded him of a friend from when he was in grad school. A guy, but also someone who was also "so American." Somehow those moments strung together—an uncanny resemblance, laughter piercing the dark, a comment from someone validating how you feel about yourself, those are the footholds offered to you when you trespass into uncomfortable territory. Maybe that's why I started talking about all this baby stuff with Oscar. Certainly some things are easier to talk to someone who doesn't already know all your baggage.

So I thought, *Why not get a reaction from Oscar, this worldly, joie de vivre-ic, beautiful, gay Colombian medical doctor living in Burma with his partner?* He was an international public health compatriot, but living a reality completely opposite from me. Sharing my deeply buried ambition with Oscar felt like dialing a boy you have a crush on before you've convinced yourself you're going to say what you want to say. I hadn't thought it through. I surprised myself with what came out.

"I want a baby, and I'm going to have one on my own." He squinted at me, then got right to the point. "How old are you?" I squinted back at him as if to say, "How old do you think I am?"

"Thirty-five in October," I admitted.

"Oh," Oscar frowned. Was it disappointment? or maybe concern? I guess he thought I was a bit younger. He took in the new information and recalculated his response. "Yes, you don't have much time. You definitely need to start thinking about making that baby." He gave me a once-over, raising his eyebrows and then a wince for emphasis. Took a drag on his cigarette and then started to laugh. It started as a giggle, then erupted into full scale cackling, then smothered itself into a deep toothy grin.

That Oscar deemed my baby plan a worthwhile endeavor suggested there was broader appeal to my plan. But it was as if he peeked over my shoulder, as I stood, age 35, one toe over the edge of the fertility cliff, and said, "Girl, that is a looooong way down."

I had to face it, looking over the edge made me feel a little sick. But one thing is for sure, you don't want going over the cliff to be some kind of accident. You can stand at the edge for a while, but you can't stand there forever. In case you didn't know, the fertility cliff is real. I've seen the graphs. I've seen the faces of health professionals conveying this information to patients, their hand like a bird face-planting into the earth, the whistling sounds coming out the sides of their mouths. For some time, I had been having conversations with girlfriends slightly older than me, in a similar work-life situation.

They were saying, "There's just nobody out there worth dating (subtext: there's no one on this site who I'd want to make babies with)."

"I don't believe in long engagements (subtext: I'm running out of time!)."

"At our age, you already know what you want (subtext: I'm not looking for a soul mate, I just want a baby!)."

"Did you hear that S— and M— got engaged?!?! (subtext: he's kind of a dope. But that's what she's gotta do if she really wants to have a baby.)."

Ending up tied to someone you didn't much like, having sex like rabbits trying to have children, and then raising them together for the next twenty plus years.... It sounded like a bad perturbation of Shag-Marry-Kill where you do all three acts to one person, and that person happens to be the father of your psychologically scarred child(ren!).

The marrying-to-make-babies type of decision-making is premised on a rigid sequence of steps: finding your life partner and then having the babies. I began to think how unnecessary that was. The ordering of the steps seemed sub-optimal when combined with a biological clock. Finding a life partner required two mutually enamored consenting adults. But not everyone might find a life partner, and it might not happen in the same time period as your preferred or bio-economically possible work-life time window. Trying to find a mate and get pregnant on a rushed time frame was akin to getting in a barrel and rolling over Niagara Falls. Why not be open to having the baby first, and then figure out the life-partner part in good time?

If you're a woman wanting to have a baby, all you really need is your own body to cooperate, a supply of quality spermatozoa, and some money saved. Those things seemed much more possible for a woman to assemble when they're ready to get pregnant. I had been told about women who had done it on their own with a sperm donor. Mostly friends of friends, not friends I knew, but I had seen pictures of these solo moms with their babies, so I knew them to be real people, not urban legends dreamed up by other over-educated, independent, professional women in my cohort. It was possible, maybe probable, to get a baby this way. A real enough possibility that I could now say I want a baby and set an intention. (Take three measured steps back from the cliff, turn, raise my arms above my head, swing them back and then take off, with a well practiced run and powerful two-footed jump off the edge, pike, double twist, hands clasped for a splashless entry.)

After agreeing with Oscar that I needed to get moving, and to stop breathing in his second-hand smoke, I took a step back from the cliff. I'll start when I turn 35, I told myself. I had a few more months to go. Okay, more like six weeks. But that seemed like an important amount of time to wait. I had watched enough J. Lo and Sandra Bullock rom-coms in my life to know, anything could happen in six weeks. These movies had taught me that life likes to fuck with over-educated single women in their thirties. And once committed to a path inconvenient to integrating a love interest into your life, such as becoming pregnant, that is the precise moment when your soul mate arrives at the door. As a precaution, I was waiting until 35 to start the process, just in case.

In truth, I needed to build a runway. I was not ready to start. I needed to figure out how to get it done. I was traveling 200 days of the year, feeling smug about myself for living a life free of any long-term plan, but there on a balcony overlooking a decaying Rangoon, humming "Don't Cry for Me, Burmese People," I had committed myself to a big complex plan. I needed this plan to avoid this baby project from being dashed on the asphalt below.

There were more ways to get off this fertility cliff than to just fall off or close my eyes and hide in a barrel. With the right preparation couldn't I strive to be a Mexican cliff diver, or Greg Louganis at the 1988 Olympics? But then, why dive at all? My plan could take me in a totally different direction. More like building a rocket and launching it at the moon. This would be the Mother of all plans, the kind of plan that would require the cooperation of a lot of different people and serious monetary resources and an exquisite sense of timing and that was just the beginning.

WHAT'S THE PLAN?

TALKING ABOUT MY MOONSHOT PLANNING, I remind myself that in fourth grade, I had a plan. I had it all worked out. I was going to have four children. I would wait until I was 26 to start and have them at two-year intervals. And the first ten years of child rearing I would stay home and then the second ten years I would reclaim my career and earn money to help send everyone to college without incurring debt. My children were going to have green eyes and black hair. There was no specific vision for or requirements related to the father. But I suppose there was presumption of having one, that we would be married, that he would be on board for the rest of the plan, and his recessive genes for green eyes could dominate my pure Chinese heritage.

The gaping hole of Mendelian logic notwithstanding, at the time, I remember thinking I was being rather sensible—I meant the part about waiting until 26 to start popping out the kids. I expected the years between age 22 and 26 would prove ample time to establish the roots of a career that could be picked up later in life. (Gimme a break, I was nine years old.) I thought I was being realistic, since 26 was reasonably late, but not too late to make having babies a problem. How is it that even then, I was aware that women in their thirties had problems making babies?

I think about this and further acknowledge that in fourth grade when people asked me what I wanted to be when I grew up, I alternated between saying I wanted to be an architect and a window washer for skyscrapers. The idea of architect was based on that being my favorite aunt's career and receiving a set of plastic tools with different sized hexagons cut out and curved edges with which to represent furniture and doorways and potentially Getty-style exterior walls. I sensed that with some attention to detail, I could fake a kind of artistry with those rulers, without needing to be able to draw free hand, which I could not. My fantasy of being a window washer is harder to explain. I don't even like heights. But the idea of going along in that box along the outside of tall buildings seemed athletic and daring in a way that fit with my sense of fourth grade self. It also seems plausible that I could take a break of ten years and jump back into a career of window washing without losing much in terms of climbing the career ladder, so to speak. It seems less plausible that a career of window washing would contribute enough to putting four kids through college. Though I don't really know.

So all that did not come to pass. Not one bit. But what I like about that fourth grade version of the baby plan is that it was holistic. It was not so much a baby plan as a life plan: there were babies, a partner in the background, and a career that figured out itself.

By the time I was an undergrad, my life plan spanned only ten years and got me as far as a job: get my bachelor's, go to grad school in Chemistry, finish in six years, and start a career as an industrial chemist. How's that for a dream? With that plan, I was sure I would live happily ever after. The kids and husband were in the background somewhere. There was less urgency in fleshing that out. This was more of a career plan with a side of family. The plan unraveled when I balked senior year thinking about a life confined to a lab all day. I cashed in a savings bond given to me at birth by my grandfather and bought a ticket to Thailand. In a completely unsolicited way, I sought out a professor and volunteered to work on a clinical trial he was beginning. The topic was how to prevent pregnant women from transmitting HIV to their babies. I had no idea what I was doing in Thailand or on the trial, but in those five months overseas, I figured out that I should write to Berkeley to tell them I was not going to be coming to Chemistry grad school in the fall and that I was going to New York City to become an Urban Fellow. Now that was the plan, it spanned one year and who knew where that would lead.

That first year as a City of New York Urban Fellow, I lived in a small apartment on the Upper East Side with two roommates. I took the 4, 5, 6 train 107 blocks to Worth Street and learned a lot about running operations for a large health department. I responded to letters from the public, I got tips from seasoned Pest Control officers about how to bludgeon a rat coming out of an underground nest with a baseball bat, I watched how my boss finessed the firing of a fellow Deputy Commissioner and still got invited to eat chicken livers with her at her going away party, and I figured out how to order Chinese food for white people having a working lunch. I was getting paid close to nothing, but hanging out with people who knew the City and how it worked.

One night toward the end of my second year, after working a night-time city event, I walked with a group of Fellows toward the subway. From some distance away, something blocked out the glare of taxi headlights and street lamps reflected in the wet asphalt. It was a group of men wearing long black coats. They walked down the middle of this Manhattan street like they owned it. We stopped to watch them. As they approached us, we could see in the lead was Rudy Giuliani, flanked by a Deputy Mayor or two. Bringing up the rear was a security guy, probably. They were laughing, maybe smoking. I remember it being like they were walking in fog. As they passed us, they nodded to a woman in our group. She had worked in one of their offices all through college. They moved off down the street like it was nobody's business. It was like something out of the *Untouchables*. But I also got a taste of feeling like I knew somebody who knew somebody and maybe one day I could be more than an extra.

New York City was a weird mix: racy and exciting, feudal and clannish, full of smart and odd people, dirty in many senses of the word, and most of all, there for the taking—but I sensed, not really a place for me. I was not thinking about babies back then, except for coming to terms with my own emotional infancy. I was nursing a troubled long-distance relationship, aided and abetted by cheap Delta flight coupons used to get between La Guardia and Logan airports. I remember that time mostly as being wintery and dreary. I can still feel the cold glass against my forehead staring out the window of that M60 bus, the affordable way for an Urban Fellow to get from my apartment in the Upper East Side to East Elmhurst. I remember thinking, *Why am I spending so much time on this depressing bus?* What was I doing with my life?

So as Giuliani began his heyday as the mayor of New York City, I hatched a new plan to pursue a career in public health working for a city or state health department. Somewhere not New York City. But first, I needed to go to grad school.

At 27, I was a newly minted Ph.D. in Epidemiology, I started a post-doc at CDC (the Centers for Disease Control—and Prevention, don't forget prevention!) in Atlanta through the Epidemiologic Intelligence Service (EIS). It was, historically, the training program that CDC used to turn medical officers into outbreak investigators. In the EIS program's most scintillating form, its graduates trace the source of monkey pox, avian flu, Ebola, and stop worldwide pandemics of zombie-ism. But more often, it looks for spoiled foods at community picnics and unhygienic practices in food processing plants or hospitals. This job offered me a two-year contract, there was no real plan. Nothing that included babies.

When I moved to Atlanta, I had just ended a six-year relationship. When you're in a relationship for six years in your twenties, you think it's the one. At least I did. I felt like we grew up together. He knew me really well. I knew what it would be like to have kids with him. It was a relationship where I didn't have to imagine what was going to happen to us. It was just a matter of when and where to get married, put down roots, buy a house, and have kids. I just had to finish grad school and the rest would get rolling. Then 9/11 happened. He had already left the house that morning. We were in California, three hours behind east coast time. By the time I realized what was happening the first tower had already come down. I remember going down to our apartment complex's common space TV to watch the news replay the first and second plane crashing, again and again. I was looking for someone to watch it with. I was huddled on the fake leather sofa slipping into a ball, holding myself, feeling numb and alone.

In the days and weeks that followed, I was around a lot of people, but I felt disconnected. I didn't know how to explain it. I was living with someone I considered to be my best friend and I couldn't make him understand how I felt. We were living in the same space, but somehow on different planes. The cycles of school and work and school and work, and later, I assumed, kids and work, offered a comforting, inevitable orbit for me to follow. By myself, I couldn't escape from the gravitational field of that relationship, that path. The 9/11 event was like colliding with an asteroid and getting knocked off course. It wasn't personal, but it set me spinning off.

I realized that I was just waiting to graduate the next spring, not because my life, our life, was going to start then but because I was waiting for a "natural" breaking off point of our relationship. He would still be in med school, but I would be going to do a post doc, probably at CDC. We didn't make sense anymore and we knew it. But we were waiting around for a more convenient time to go through the heartache. We were still friends. Why break up if we're going to part ways in a couple of months? Why go through the hassle of finding another place to live just as I'm trying to finish my dissertation? But I did it. That was surely a lonely, miserable way to finish a Ph.D. program. You could say that graduation would have come. We would have broken up then anyway. What made it a good idea to end it a couple of months early? It was good to face an unpleasant truth about my situation. To be okay, being alone. The universe didn't collapse in on me. And that fact turned out to be a helpful thing to know.

I envisioned my move to Atlanta as a kind of migrating back to the East Coast for a reboot in my personal life. I was horrified to realize that Atlanta was not actually coastal and mortified by my poor sense of geography. It was also dismaying to find out despite the presence of eminent organizations such as CDC, CNN, and Coca Cola, cosmopolitan Atlanta also vied for title as the strip-club capital of the United States. It seemed an unlikely place for me to put down roots. My work assignment with the Global AIDS Program promised to have me overseas for at least a third to half of the days of the year. My friends at CDC were in their mid to late thirties—they were buying houses and having kids, in addition to starting or restarting careers after grad school. They said I was still a baby. They told me to use condoms and enjoy life. "Fuck your old boyfriends," if you felt like it. They laughed, remembering their old lives; when lots of parameters were still open, when there were still several wild cards in the deck, waiting to be turned over.

My job at the CDC included me becoming part of the Commissioned Corps. As part of the uniformed services, we were under the command of the Surgeon General. We should be ready to re-deploy faster than someone could say, "salmonella." My commission came with a uniform allowance and I purchased a standard wool-poly blend navy dress blue. Custom alterations were included in the cost of the uniform, but for me, there was no tailoring required. I fit the standard size perfectly. I took it as a sign that I was meant to be a part of this organization. This particular material they used to fabricate uniforms had the surface texture of cat scratched neoprene. It melded to my body as I walked across the blistering parking lot that serviced a group of satellite CDC offices and the Pink Pony strip club. In my uniform, I felt fully prepared to don a scuba tank and dive to the bottom of the ocean looking for pathogens, as needed.

I am saying, for once in my life I was very happy to be in the service of a higher authority and carry out assignments and not think about my personal bigger picture. Redeployment was always a possibility. When I signed up for the Corps, I had to be okay with circumstances that could completely disrupt how I lived and worked, in order to respond to an urgent need. It was fun to both totally invest in the task at hand and be ready to drop it because your supreme leader determined that you were needed elsewhere and should be doing something else. (If you didn't know, the Corps supreme leader is the Surgeon General, who was at the time literally a surgeon and a general appointed by George W. Bush. And we used to joke that George Bush was too dense to understand the qualifications to be the head of the Corps. I suppose, in reality, Bush was the Supreme Leader, but it was then and still is hard to acknowledge that as part of the deal.) I never belonged to a cult or even a sports team. I had earlier been skeptical about the role of the military as an instrument of war. But there was something secretly appealing to being part of a quasi-military organization, expressing loyalty to a larger cause than my own ambition. For a time, it was an excuse not to worry about the long-term plan.

At the end of our two-year EIS program, my cohort of medical epidemiologists applied for promotions in rank and jockeyed for permanent positions in the agency. People were ready to climb the ladder from being section leader, to team leader, to branch chief, maybe skipping straight to center director. At the very least, people were counting on doing 20 years and then cashing in on a pension. It was tempting, I gravitated toward getting on that track.

Instead, I quit my job at CDC. I shed the uniform, but kept the mantle of being free of big plans for myself. That still felt good for the time being.

I took a job overseas in India. And then two years after that, I quit that job and went independent as a public health consultant. There was still no real plan, except that I could do things solo and I learned to take care of things myself.

I have always depended on the kindness of strangers—it almost came out of my mouth. But I stopped myself. Few would say that I was the Blanche DuBois type, certainly not the way Vivien Leigh played her. But I was not above adopting a bit of a drawl. As I climbed into the back of a dark SUV to sit next to a strange man at the Benazir Bhutto International

Airport in Islamabad, I thought to myself, *Maybe I am a bit mentally unstable.*

It was September 2008. I had just spent an uneasy week holed up at a fortress on a hill, otherwise known as the Serena Hotel. To approach the hotel, a car had to snake at five miles per hour through a narrow, barricade-lined path that looked like a go-cart track, a tower of guards perched above with automatic weapons ready to gun down suspicious vehicles, as needed. Once a car got through that stage and was thoroughly searched, then it could park. Guests would get out, get the once over, and either transfer themselves to a hotel car to ascend another steep driveway, or self-actualize up four flights of steps through a concrete tunnel to reach the hotel lobby. Self-consciously, I almost always took the stairs.

Once inside the lobby, there were thick jewel toned carpets and chandeliers twinkling to classical music greats. If it weren't for the razor wire and the guns, the hotel could have been mistaken for a fairy castle in the clouds. It's hard to imagine an architect would design such a thing in Islamabad except for the purposes of making expats feel secure staying in such a place. Though the World Bank housed its consultants at the Serena, they hired tired, low-to-the-ground Corollas, unlikely to be IED-proof vehicles, with friendly, lackadaisical drivers to shuttle those on mission back and forth from the hotel to the office.

I was nervous to be in Pakistan. Benazir Bhutto had been assassinated the year before. That is a bad time to go to a country, when they just renamed their airport to commemorate a recently assassinated leader. Usually I like to wait for at least two years after that happens before visiting. I had not told my family where I was going. I figured that it would make them worry, so I made up some story about going to a meeting in Bangkok. I made it through the week without a terrorist incident, and was dropped off at the airport, but after waiting twenty minutes in the check-in line, the airline announced that the flight had been canceled and would not be rescheduled until at least the next day.

The travelers around me looked annoyed, but for me, panic began to set in. There I was—no cell phone, my ghetto getaway car long gone from the terminal. I was fully checked out of my hotel. As far as the Bank was concerned, I was onward to the next mission on behalf of WHO. It wasn't clear how much responsibility they took for consultants who had turned in their mission reports and surrendered their visitor badges.

My instinct was to go find refuge in the castle on the hill, and do some comfort eating—it wouldn't hurt to have a little more of the hotel's excellent mutton biriyani. After all, when would I be back again? But the official security briefing I had received before arrival warned consultants not to get into a local taxi. So how was I supposed to get myself back to the Serena?

I surveilled the assembled group of fellow canceled flight passengers and put my bets on the one white guy. He seemed irritated, but nonplussed. He was wearing jeans and a turtleneck under a nondescript gray fleece. He had a cell phone and a North American accent. I made my way over to him. From what I could make out, he was calling his driver who didn't seem that far away. I summoned my inner Blanche DuBois, "Excuse me, Sir, you're not by chance going to the Serena. Are you?" I don't know why I addressed him as "Sir." An effort to ingratiate myself a little more, maybe. People had addressed me as Madame all week, so it probably didn't strike him as so odd.

He looked at me and sized me up. I could have passed for an Indonesian maid, but my accent was decidedly American. I tried to look single and charmingly nervous, without seeming completely unhinged.

"No," he said, "but I can give you a lift. My driver will be here in a few minutes."

I tried to be a bit chirpy while we waited for the car, a small glass of sparkling conversation to make the favor of a ride worthwhile. "Are you based in Islamabad? This is my first time in the country. It's not what I expected...at all." It was a neutral opener, intended to be compatible with however positively or negatively he felt about Pakistan, but promising I had my own opinion. On the curb, he appeared to be a small talk teetotaler. But in the car, he told me he was a military consultant, his name was Joe, he was a retired Marine. He said the place was going to shit, security was getting worse every day, and the Serena was actually the last place you wanted to be, because it was sitting on the hill like a beacon to terrorists looking for soft targets, i.e. a watering hole for affluent expats.

He said the last part as we were snaking through the Serena's go-cart track. I looked at him to see if he was joking. It was kind of a mean thing to say to someone as you're dropping them off at said terrorist beacon, and in what felt like slow-motion. He let it sink in as we approached the death trap. I almost reluctantly let the car door shut behind me. Before I could turn around to wave and again convey my thanks, the car sped away toward what I imagined was his own safe house. In a different frame of mind, I would have chalked it up to him being a security guy. All of those embassy security guys are the same. They tell you that every foreign national you meet wants to bed you because they want to use you to get state secrets. They tell you if an explosive goes through a plate glass window the shards would shear your body in half, just like that. Their attitude is: they can't really protect you from those kinds of hazards, but it's their obligation to let you know that it can happen. My best chance for survival was to pay attention to their rules and follow them as told.

When my plane actually left Islamabad, while it still felt like there was a stone in my gut, I told myself there would be no next time. Not just about going back to Pakistan, but I should really think things through better and not put myself in the position of being forced to rely on others. Because relying on others, whether strangers or otherwise, felt bad. I could give myself a pass in times of natural disasters or actual terrorist events. But not when I could have been prepared.

Within only a few months of life as a public health consultant, I figured out I just needed good internet and a convenient airport and I could be anywhere. So I bought a house in Hilo, a town I had never lived in, where I started out only knowing an entomologist who worked intermittently with my mother; my well-connected realtor; and one friend of an aunt who was part time on-island. Good thing there were a lot of transient people in Hilo, many other people with no long-term plan. People were low key and friendly. Hilo is the kind of place where if you're walking in your neighborhood and you stop to admire some flowering bush in somebody's yard, they will come out running with a pair of clippers and ask if they can give you a cutting. (That really happened to me early on living in Hilo. Hilo is also the kind of place that if you stick something in the ground, more often than not it will just grow. So consequently, I have a really cool looking hibiscus growing in my yard. It has a small red flower with a white poodle-tail stamen. I named it Lucy.) Hilo is at once a lush and stark place; it feels both new-age and primal. You can stand on undulating lava rock immersed in the ocean and look up to a snow-capped mountain crowned with telescopes that are tuned upward toward the rest of the galaxy. That kind of vista makes you feel privy to an infinite line of time and space. I surprised myself by living in Hilo, longer than I had ever lived anywhere since going away to college. It was the perfect home base to return to after grueling work travel in foreign places.

Hilo was less ideal as a cosmos of dating. I didn't have family or a big network of friends there. I didn't go to an office to work. So the people I met initially, the sum of my dating scene, mostly consisted of people I had hired to perform various services on my home and car: my yard guy (he offered to do my lawn for free), my mechanic (an encounter set up by his mother, who was a friend of my realtor), a flirty, very talkative electrician (he turned out to be married and had two kids enrolled in the Keikiland down the street). I drew the line at a chronically late and overcharging contractor, even though he seemed interested and legitimately single.

Early on, I had tried the online dating thing. I had criteria I thought were reasonable, but being on a rural island, preferring men within five years of my age, who lived on-island, and did not already have children turned out to be unrealistic. In retrospect, it seems hypocritical to have excluded people who already had children, but at that time, my thinking hadn't quite evolved. And serves me right, because I suspect that criterion, no prior children, had effectively limited the pool to almost nothing. All the more so when you are looking for a life partner, not just a hookup.

But there were a handful of options and I gave it a go. One guy didn't have as many teeth in the front as his profile picture suggested. Another guy spoke really softly and mostly talked about hating his job and wanting to move back to Moloka'i. A third guy, also quiet, talked about doing Peace Corps and wishing he had kept in touch with the people he met in Paraguay. These guys were wistful about their pasts and seemed disempowered to do reasonably doable things. I was not sure why that was. And I wasn't that interested in finding out. I did meet one reasonably active person who seemed enthused about playing tennis and scoping out good plate lunch places afterward. If I hadn't found a real match, at least I might have found an activity partner, I thought. But then he got a job off island and that was that. Soon, all the work my house and car needed were done and I let my Match.com account lapse.

And that is how I ended up in Rangoon talking to Oscar about having babies on my own. Why I had to have this do-it-yourself plan.

Who's Your Daddy?

It was a big decision to pursue having a baby on my own. Life would have been simpler if I had been in a stable, loving relationship. It would have been simpler if I were a parthenogenic Komodo dragon, for that matter. But as Pema Chödrön advises, touch that stinky, uncomfortable reality for a moment. Wholly commit to where you are in the present moment.

Having made my decision, it was a relief to know that the rest was just a matter of logistics.

I'm a planning type. Logistics are everything to me. Planning is my art. It is my science. It is my religion. Logistics seem tactical but at a deep level it brings me clarity and comfort. It is an easy mental space for me to be in.

First up, I needed to figure out who or how to father this child. A large decision tree suddenly sprang up in front of me. At this stage it still felt like the land of magical thinking, so maybe I should describe it more as a giant beanstalk leading into the clouds. A beanstalk I had sown by throwing the crazy seed of having a baby by myself out my window. What do you do when you wake up and find something like that has rooted outside your door? You just start climbing, stepping crotch by crotch until you get to the top. Somehow that seems like the right imagery to conjure up.

The first decision on the way up was choosing whether this baby was going to be made via a known donor or an anonymous donor. Was I going to review my email contact list or look through a binder full of men at some reputable sperm bank? My gut said sperm bank. It seemed a cleaner choice. Literally, the sperm came pre-washed. More importantly, it offered a way to maintain a total sense of control over the process. I thought it best to have a highly mediated relationship with a donor, keep it professional and outcome oriented. I hoped to avoid any emotional creep. Paying for the service seemed necessary in order to accomplish that.

Impenetrable anonymity was another option offered by the use of a sperm bank (at the time). Some donors left open the opportunity to be contacted later, others did not. I wasn't considering the donor a new person in my life. The word "donor" made things seem nicely disembodied. I started off certain that the best arrangement was a fully anonymous one.

It was clearly the best arrangement for me anyway, but what if my kid felt differently?

"Who's my daddy?" my little girl might ask suddenly over French toast in the morning.

"Uhhhh. I have no idea." I'd have to say. Then resort to a diversionary tactic. "Now eat up your breakfast or you'll be late for school." That scenario felt pretty lame. I could see this lack of conversation leading to a lifetime of unrest in my child's sense of self. This was the reality check for my needing to consider more than my own comfort in this endeavor. Choosing a knowable or anonymous donor: the first test of good parenting started even before conception.

I began thinking it through in detail. There were health-related reasons that make being able to contact a donor in the future a good idea. But with technology these days, maybe most of those things could be figured out with a DNA test. What would I do if my kid wanted to find their donor? What if that person turned out to be a jerk?

I went back and forth with the pros and cons of each option. I talked to friends who had gone through open adoptions and couldn't imagine it any other way. I read books about bi-racial kids searching for decades to find their American GI fathers. I skimmed articles about adult Korean kids rejecting their adopted American parents in search of their true parentage, homeland, and culture. Things were leaning in the direction of your kids will hate you forever if you stand in the way of them knowing their biological parents. Then I watched the *Kids Are All Right*. And on the basis of potentially having a late life affair with a Mark Ruffalo-like character, I was convinced I should definitely go for an open sperm donor.

I came to an important realization about myself. I was all-in to be the inspiration for a Netflix Original Series. Here's another crazy baby making scheme to help people learn about their possibilities. Based on a true story—but with snappier dialog and maybe a little more fortuitous sex. David Kelly, Shonda Rhimes, Tina Fey, Mindy Kaling—let's talk.

Donor decision-making made things slippery. Finding reasonable footholds in magical bean stalks is tough. I thought I was approaching things from a very concrete and rational perspective, but I was surprised by the degree of difficulty in making decisions. Usually I am very good at making decisions. I had had a minor breakdown and bout of depression my sophomore year in high school, and the advice I got from my dean was not to regret decisions, just recognize your mistakes and keep moving forward trying to correct them as best you can. And really that has saved me a ton of heartache.

It certainly has served me well in making monetary decisions, which are 90% of the hard decisions I've had to make. I'm talking about choosing colleges, job opportunities, eye wear, and large appliances. I scan my options and then go with my gut. I don't balk, I just choose. As a rule of thumb, with the exception of higher education, I go with the second-most cheap option. And then I make whatever happens okay.

The stakes involved with choosing a sperm donor from a sperm bank are higher. It's not the same as finding a yard guy or contractor or electrician. Your yard guy could kill your favorite hibiscus, or your contractor could do a bad tile job. Those things can be fixed. A sperm donor is your sperm donor forever. No backsies. You want to check them out before you choose, but you don't want sperm donors with Yelp reviews, you don't want to use the same guy your friend went to. With an open donor, there was a possibility this person could become a fixture in your emotional life, sit next to you at your kid's graduation, dance at your child's wedding. Thinking about the serious implications of my choice not just for myself but for my family, more and more this was feeling like an arranged marriage: picking someone you've never met on the basis of idealized characteristics, with potentially lifelong consequences.

(It is useful at this point to recognize extreme privilege as a precursor to even contemplating these types of decisions. Being born in the right place and at the right time. It goes beyond having a safety net if I were to lose my livelihood, or had health complications. It's also about making decisions for yourself that impact the people around you. I've had conversations with women who I thought were in the same situation as me: working in the same field, educated, economically self-sustaining, with close family, but who are not able to think about having kids on their own, or through artificial technology. It's just not an acceptable choice in some groups. Just like love-marriage, or inter-religious dating, or choosing Mac over PC.)

Arghh, I went back and forth on this decision, I couldn't fully come down on one side or the other about anonymous donor or not. At least, I could decide it was going to be a paid donor, certainly not someone I knew. Relying on that firm footing was a way to move forward.

So what were these qualities in a donor that I was looking for? Finally, some easy, fun decisions to make in this process. It was like being in fourth grade again—thinking what color hair and eyes I wanted my baby to come with. I stepped out of the dread of arranged-marriage decision making, I was ready to swipe right and swipe left using a cheeky online app to indicate my preferences. I wanted someone tall, athletic, smart. But how did I indicate a desire for someone funny, easy-going, and a bit of a goofball. Filling in this donor request form was just like filling in the questionnaire of an online dating profile. Only better. It was a power trip to get to say what you wanted without any pressure to market yourself as a compatible or mutually desirable match.

And then this feeling like the start of some major indigestion started to creep in. It felt like a burning in my chest. Right in that tender muscle on the left, you know, that thing called the heart. Was I picking attributes to be passed down to my biological child, or was I picking a fantasy life partner with whom to have a child? My heart cringed, it knew that the pleasure elicited from choosing the genetic attributes of my child, was an expensive consolation prize for not finding a mate who had these same qualities and who was available or interested in me. *Blahck*.

This heart burn would persist.

And then I began to think, *What does making this list really say about me?* First, it says I'm shallow, if not racist. My first considerations for the donor were all physical characteristics. Hair and eye color might be innocuous, but what about complexion. When you're picking a lover, you may have a preference for a certain look, whether you label it as "I like white guys" or black guys or whatever guys. It's up to you. You can claim that's just what you find attractive. And then what happens if you meet an interesting guy who looks different than "your type?" Sometimes that happens. And then, if you end up having kids, you get what you get. If you have kids that way, you don't say, "I would prefer one that looks lighter, that has blue eyes, and is smart." So much for parental unconditional love, if you state up front you prefer characteristics that your kid may or may not end up having.

My mother told us kids once that my father really wouldn't mind having dumb kids. I couldn't figure out what she meant. I thought about it for a long time. Did she mean if we weren't too bright, Daddy wouldn't love us less? I was skeptical about that. It didn't seem right. I couldn't imagine how he could love dumb kids. They would be dumb! Then I started thinking, maybe she meant he would love us more if we were dumb. Did he want dumb kids, because maybe they would be simple and sweet, and not pose challenges, so it would be easier to be their dad? I saw myself as a serious child who had complex feelings. Sometimes, like lots of kids, I felt less than I wanted to be—shorter, not a fast runner, I wore glasses, I got really dark if I was out in the sun. Maybe dumb kids had it good because they were loved more and didn't know they were dumb, so they didn't feel bad about themselves. I think the moral of that story is don't let your kids know you could love other kinds of kids as much as you love them. True or not, no matter what you meant, that's not helpful information for them to know.

At first, verbalizing the characteristics I wanted in a donor felt different than specifying the kind of kid I wanted. But I began to realize that was convenience thinking. If you check that box for white guy, there's no chance (okay, maybe actually a small chance) your baby will end up with a donor that's anything but. One part of myself wanted to boycott the check boxes in the donor demographics form. I sat with that idea for a bit. It's great to say, all I want is a kid who is intelligent, liberal in politics, civic minded, and doesn't have a history of schizophrenia, heart disease or diabetes. I could believe that with warm authoritative parenting, early childhood education, augmented by a good diet and exercise, I could take care of all those things. It's not important to me what the donor looks like or where he went to school. That feels really righteous, right on. But on the other hand, leaving those boxes blank also felt crazy; doing that was "not keeping it real."

It's like when I was in sixth grade and I announced to my mother, "I think it's kind of sexist to say you're only attracted to men or women. Shouldn't I just be looking for a nice person who I get along with, regardless if they are a male or female?"

And my mother put down the knife she was using to prepare dinner, and took a look at me and nodded, then said, "Well, it's obvious you've never had sex." Then she went back to her chopping. At the time, I didn't really see what that had to do with anything. But now I get it. Desire comes from a deep place, what we want is not always what we're supposed to want. What we want is not always what we get. But we want it anyway. And if we are given the opportunity to have it, it seems disingenuous not to reach for it.

Now, I imagined my mother standing next to me holding a knife asking, "Are you really going to leave all those boxes unchecked as a matter of principle?" Had she raised some kind of fool? After all the money and all the effort I was about to put into this endeavor, was I really not going to state a preference. It wasn't being true to my deep down inside I-really-want-to-have-a-(certain-kind-of)-baby-self.

If you asked my mother what she was looking for way back when, what she was looking for in a mate, I wonder if she could describe it. I asked my mother once what she found attractive about my father when they were first dating. He was a guy from Hawaiʻi—a third-generation born in America kind of Chinese. Unlike most of the Chinese guys she had met at the University of Illinois, Champagne-Urbana, he was a native English speaker, and identified as 100% American; nothing like the kids from Hong Kong my mother mainly hung out with at the student union on the Illini campus. My father would arrive at her house on a bicycle to pick her up for dates. He carried roasted peanuts in the shell in his pocket, and offered them to her as they walked to the movies. He had thick black hair and was tall for an Asian guy. Were those the reasons? No. She said she noticed he had good, strong teeth. Had he been a black man, there might have been an outcry of "racism!" But he was a Chinese guy, and if you saw his teeth, you might remark yourself that they were large and well formed. Nothing weak or insipid about them. I think my father's teeth signified a stable childhood of good nutrition, access to adequate calcium and protein, not to mention routine health care.

My mother grew up in Vietnam, after her family escaped the Japanese invasion of China. Then with the Vietnam war, they had to emigrate again, to America, to be safe. With his teeth, my dad advertised the stability and belonging my mother might have wanted for her kids. My mother might not have elected to climb a magical invasive species and steal a golden egg from a giant named *Traditional Lifestyle*, aka *Patriarchy*. But when given the choice, she had effectively checked the boxes on a donor form that said Chinese, tall, and highly educated.

All Natural

THERE'S MORE TO SPERM DONORS than the characteristics listed on a profile. I started reading more about sperm donors. I found all these articles about sperm donors who donated—a lot! Some of these men seemed to have super potent sperm; their spermatozoa practically leaping out of the vials into women's uteruses. Plus, these donors had many appealing characteristics, e.g. athletic builds and good professional jobs, and maybe a higher degree, maybe an Ivy League pedigree, so a lot of women wanted this super-duper sperm. In some cases, there were donors with fifty, sixty, possibly hundreds of children. And because sperm donation was largely local, i.e. the women choosing these donors lived in the same local area, there were possibly many children who were half siblings who lived near each other, maybe went to school together, and possibly could one day meet and date each other and never know that they were related. *Agggghhh.* This threw a wrench into things.

There must be statistics on this. You would think clinics kept records on how many times a sperm donor's stuff had been used; how many times this resulted in a live birth. Clinics had to track success rates, but did they keep databases on patients and outcomes in a way they could analyze their data in reasonable ways or did someone just keep track with a tick mark on a piece of paper? Donor success rate is a double-edged sword. For some people, a low rate meant a lower likelihood that their child would be part of a large network of who knows how many half-siblings. But a high rate of success meant hearty, vigorous sperm which could traverse even the most hostile uterine environment. Potent sperm meant fewer expensive attempts to implant and have a successful pregnancy. But on top of all these calculated risks, could you really rely on the clinic's data to know true success rates if donors contributed to multiple sperm banks in the area?

And so, I began to wonder about the motivation of these people donating buckets of their life juices to others. Making money was an understandable reason, perhaps the best reason, though it would seem to correlate to large and frequent donation. Altruism was another reason, but it was hard to think of a back story in which sperm donation made sense as a significant way to express feelings of altruism. Having a Genghis Khan complex was possible and disturbing. Just being a weirdo was a reason which encompassed most everything else I could come up with.

And then, through the powers of the internet, I found Trent. Here was a guy who claimed "altruism" as his motivation. He was so altruistic that he didn't charge money for his goods. Perhaps donating goods does not adequately describe his mission; Trent may have seen himself more as a service provider. Whatever the case, his goods and services were free and for the taking/requesting. Trent had his own website, on which he posted his lab results showing that he had sperm count and motility levels that were standards of deviation above normal. His website also had a handy calendar from which you could sign up for the dates of your free vials. And by free, I mean, that even the vial itself was free. Which Trent supplied at his own expense; this form of generosity was something he emphasized on his website.

I was so curious and fixated on what could possibly motivate Trent to do this. So I read his website in much detail, looked at the pictures of the women and their children who claimed to be Trent success stories. There were testimonials from women who could not have afforded to have their children any other way, and thanked God for Trent and his generous spirit. And then I read the instructions on the calendar portion of the website which said that once a person, presumably a woman, had signed up for the day and time they wished to receive their Trent-sperm, that they should send a reminder text message 15 minutes before the pick-up time. This would ensure Trent had enough time to "prepare" the specimen.

Stop there. Don't think too hard about what that might involve. Move on to the next sentence. And then when said woman arrived at Trent's house, she should look for a special mailbox on the side of his garage. And in this mailbox, still warm, nested in a clean paper towel would be, sealed in a sterile (free!) vial, would be an aliquot of Trent's guys. *Ugh.* Clearly, there were really only two reasons to do this, to make money and because you are a weirdo.

Who were the women who were using Trent-sperm, I wondered. Were they not reading the same website I was reading? How come they weren't feeling that same sick feeling I was feeling? Wasn't it clear to them that something was not right, not normal about this guy? What was going on in their minds? Maybe the women using Trent-sperm were being straight with themselves, recognizing that the whole thing was not a normal thing for them to do, the whole wanting to have a child without a male partner, to obtain a donor's sperm and to impregnate themselves, by themselves. If you thought about it that way, maybe it didn't matter what Trent's motivations were. Didn't the ends justify the means? According to this website there were many women with happy ends. The subtext of the website was don't ask too many questions, sign up on the calendar, send the text and pick up the goods at the appointed hour.

I had to ask myself, how badly did I want my baby? What if I didn't have the means to afford a sperm donor, would I just give up the idea of having a baby on my own? What made me different from the Trent-sperm women? Maybe I was the same as them, I just didn't want to admit it to myself. Was I committed to this idea of having a baby? Was I going to let an unorthodox system of collecting a sperm donation so easily deter me? Instead of questioning Trent's motivations, should I really be questioning my own level of dedication to this process?

Later, it would come out that the FDA requested that Trent cease and desist his service. Because it was not hygienic. Technically, they couldn't stop him for just being creepy. But Trent appealed because he was not charging people for the specimen, so asked, on what basis could the FDA regulate him. In the controversy that followed, CNN got the scoop that Trent was a virgin and yet he had fathered an unknown, large number of children. How's that for the immaculate conception story, turned on its head?

This whole Trent situation made me rethink things. I was committed to the idea of having a baby on my own, and a baby of myself, i.e. I wanted to conceive and deliver it, go through the whole process of pregnancy. So, I was committed, but I also decided I felt completely unsettled with the many, many unknowns of an unknown donor.

I dropped back down to the start and instead made my way along the branch of thinking labeled "known donor." Instead of looks, race, and what kind of job they had, for all its added complications, I was now looking for someone whom I knew well, and whose idiosyncrasies I already appreciated, someone who was motivated because they wanted to help me, someone who would find jacking off on a schedule dictated by the request of strangers as uninteresting and possibly offensive, but would do it a limited number of times if really necessary, for a good friend. Oh, and I almost forgot, I also wanted autonomy in how I raised this child. Everyone should be clear; I was looking for a sperm donor not a co-parent. That was a set of criteria that implied many other things about the person, but on paper these were criteria I could feel good about.

In the end my operational criteria were: someone I could have a frank personal conversation with and someone I could imagine having in my life for the rest of my life. I also had the instinct that it would be better to ask someone who wasn't in a current long-term relationship, someone who didn't already have children. This was based on the idea that making this decision wouldn't be easy for an individual, let alone if they had members of a nuclear family that also needed to be considered/consulted in order to commit to the project. That was just my sense of logistics poking its way into the process.

Did I know anybody that had these attributes and would I be able to ask them to do this for me? I needed more than a single anybody, I needed to come up with a list of people to ask, because it was likely that a bunch of men were going to turn me down. How was this not less complicated than finding a life partner? How was this not going to be as demoralizing as online dating?

I wanted men who were likely to want to do it, so I could reduce the possibility of being turned down. After many rejections, I might chicken out or lose my confidence to keep asking. It was also clear that these were somewhat perpendicular axes: the x-axis being their enthusiasm for being my known donor; the y-axis being how being their desirability as a candidate to provide the sperm for my child;

People who were too willing to do it, struck me as a little odd. It turned out to be an inverted U-shaped curve. It ended up being a short list, even without adding geographical boundaries. But I got my list. Trent did not make the list. He only qualified on the first criterion. Based on that test case, I figured that my criteria were doing the job. Now all I had to do was figure out how to do the asking.

Would you be surprised if I told you I am the kind of person who maps out imaginary conversations with other people? If my mind were projected onto a screen, the title slide would read, "popping the question" and then underneath it in bullets: set the tone, bring up a hypothetical, continue to probe. The next slide would be a flow chart. You get the idea.

But that's not how it works in real life. That's just crazy talk in my head.

I didn't even know where to start on my list of potential donors. Do you make a list in the order you most hoped a person would say, "Yes!"? Then do you start at the top of the list? Why not go for your number one choice and work your way down the list as you got rejected?

If you were paying attention earlier, the pattern probably goes: the person who has the qualities you most want in a provider of sperm, is also more likely to reject you. So, do you order your list according to whom you would most like to say "Yes?" But what if the first person on that list is someone you get a queasy feeling about. Do you even put people on your list who meet the criteria but that you feel a little dread when you think about having their baby?

Or do you treat this search as if you are looking to cast a part, start with a longer list of applicants, consider people who may be a bit out of the box, do an initial round of meet-ups and then tell people, congratulations you're on the short list. That was a poor way to envision this process. I was pretty sure I should not let potential donors know there were multiple people on the list. How would you tell someone you decided to go with someone else for the part? You only need to run the mortifyingly awkward conversation through your head once to realize you wouldn't be able to look that person in the eye and explain it. Erection! Objection. Rejection?!? Who wants to get rejected for a part they didn't really want in the first place?

So much for people I wouldn't mind having in my life for the rest of my life. I could easily make everyone I knew who was list-adjacent super uncomfortable to be around me: by asking them and then rejecting them, asking them and being rejected by them, or not asking them thereby implying pre-rejection.

What I had in my hand was a wish list, not a list of candidates. I was making the pitch and the person I asked had to think they were my first choice and possibly my only hope for bearing a child. This was a search more akin to head hunting. I needed to make some discreet inquiries. I was going to approach people who had not been looking for the job. Who might have been surprised they were being considered. Who had to take a leap of faith and be willing to take a risk. And then hopefully I could close the deal.

If I asked someone, I had to be prepared to go all the way. At least on my end of things. The donor, presumably, could back out at any time, that was something I made a mental note to emphasize when I got to a certain point of the conversation. It was part of the hard sell. No risk involved. You can always back out if you feel uncomfortable or your situation changes. No risk involved. Who was I kidding? Thinking about that guarantee now, I admit that was a bit disingenuous. If my donor had decided to back out, I'm sure I would do many regrettable things to get them to reconsider. Though at the time, it was a principle I tried to assure my potential candidates of. Honestly, I will take care of everything. All you have to do is supply the sperm. Really, I, we, nobody will ask you for anything else in the future. Ever.

Despite thinking all this through, at least up to that point, I did the opposite. I didn't go with my list, ordered one way or another. I was too scared. I asked someone who wasn't on the list. Someone I didn't know well enough to be able to tell if he qualified to be on the list. He was someone I had met in Afghanistan. Actually, by the time I asked him, he had just moved to Dubai. By that time, technically, I had known him for two and a half years. Though in truth, we were in the same geographic location maybe only seven weeks total during that time and I never talked to him when we weren't in the same place. We didn't email or iChat either. But I asked him. Almost outright. We weren't good enough friends for me to lure him into a conversation about a girlfriend trying to have a baby by herself. Truly, we had no mutual friends. It was hard to describe him as a friend to begin with. He was someone I knew. He was fun to hang out with in an otherwise dismal work locale. I called him every time I was in town, that town being Kabul.

He met many of my criteria. He was clearly not in a relationship. He didn't have children, though he said he liked them. It seemed unlikely that he was going to have any anytime soon. He was probably 45. But what else did I know about him? I liked his sense of humor; he was somewhat of an adventurer. In Kabul, he planted rose bushes and grape vines in the courtyard of the compound where he took up residence. I smiled and out of the blue asked him. And he smiled back and said without much pause, "My sperm are too old." He said he had read an article that said men with old sperm make defective babies. And then that was that, we started talking about something else. I think he knew I was serious, though I brought it up so casually. And I think his answer was serious. Or at least it was a firm no, with a graceful exit.

You would think that I would have stopped there and reverted back to my original, carefully thought-out strategy. But I did it again. There had been another person I had been pursuing across international borders. A guy I had first met in Africa, and then caught up with again in the Mediterranean. And there was a moment after a really good plate of mezze and a decent piece of baklava, when I thought, *Oh maybe this could work.* As in the larger cosmic way. But why that prompted me to ask is beyond me. Did I think that was going to be a charming entry into a more serious relationship? Clearly, I had let the moment get the best of me. But in the spirit of what, at the time, was a casual relationship, I asked in a casual way. And he said back, equally casually, that it was his general policy to know the children he had produced. And that seemed to be a larger commentary on what this relationship was. Clearly, he wasn't expecting to see much of me in the future, which obviated the ability to see said progeny, therefore it was a no go. I was a little disappointed at the time, more about the relationship than the no child left behind policy. For some reason, I didn't take it as personally as I probably should have.

It all seems so, well, casual—unusual for someone who, in general, is not very casual. I am planned, I am serious, and yet, there were these two aberrant casual relationships in my recent history, and I had been compelled to ask both of them if they were willing to make a child with me. Not intuitive. Was there something in my biology, perhaps their major histocompatibility complexes that I was attracted to because they had good genetics? Was my subconscious saying that I really wanted a donor who would be very unlikely to interfere in the future life of raising my child? Maybe I just felt like posing the impossible question to people with whom I knew it was impossible because it seemed so difficult to ask the people who might actually consider the question more seriously. Or maybe it was because it was so hard to get into a relationship with these men, that it seemed no more unlikely that they would donate sperm. Because that was how hard it felt to find a life partner. Why not pile it on all at once? Consider donating your sperm, and if you like the way I raise our child, maybe you would consider a long-term relationship. Otherwise, no risk, just walk away.

It seemed crazy and contradictory. I was freestyling and it was just the beginning of this whole process. I had a plan. I had criteria. I had a strategy—why couldn't I just stick to the diagrams?

As I consider it in retrospect, both those times the question came out of my mouth organically, without premeditation. There was something satisfying about the way it sounded. It was a crisp pop as when you are cleaning asparagus, trying to get rid of the woody stem. You bend the stalk and there is a natural point where the stem is tender enough to make a clean break. You don't have to think too hard or know where exactly, it happens by itself.

Natural and easy though it was, I was still 0 for 2 in getting a donor. Part of the trouble was that I lived in Hawai'i, and that means the closest man on the official list was more than 2500 miles away. That was good for raising a child with autonomy, but not so good for heart-to-heart conversations and getting this process moving.

A few months after coming up with the list, I had a conversation with my dad about finding a sperm donor. He had asked, "How are things going?", checking in on how close the whole crazy plan was to fruition. He asked as if the subject were progress on the raised beds in my garden. As if I were trying to grow tomatoes instead of creating babies. As if my biggest challenge were handling slugs or thrips. He might have some advice to offer if that's all it was.

He is a good father. I give him a lot of credit for engaging the topic proactively.

I was explaining that it was hard to figure out who to ask, let alone how to ask. And that sometimes I was tempted to try to trick people out of their sperm. Ha, ha, ha, he laughed, a real belly laugh, how could you trick someone out of their sperm? It seemed inconceivable to him. Like the outrageous schemes of the Coyote against the Road Runner or Sylvester catching Tweety. Suffering succotash, that sperm eludes me! Maybe because at this point, the donor route, which is all I had talked about, seemed so clinical, so sterile. There were supposed to be laboratories and people with white coats and instruments involved. It did not occur to him, it seems, that at this point a known donor could still technically be a sex partner.

The male friends, whom I had talked to about finding a donor, people who were not on my list, expressed incredulity that I was making it so difficult.

"Why do you have to be so up front about it?"

"How hard is it to find someone who's willing to have sex?"

"Why do they have to know? Accidents happen."

"Get some sex, have a kid. Win-win."

What I got out of those conversations is that men don't really know how to think about having babies. For these guys, it was par for the course for women to trick men into have babies. That made me sad. The whole point of having a known donor was the possibility that my child would want to know the father. I needed someone who would not be problematic to introduce to my child. Begetting babies with men who were easily tricked or just plain careless seemed a bad beginning. How do you explain how it happened to your child, or your parents, your sister, or any of your friends? Having sex with random men whom you don't care enough about to mind tricking them into making a child seemed almost as bad as making an appointment with Trent's garage.

I was not closer to making this baby plan come to fruition. Month by month I was getting older and less fertile. As I told myself many times in this process: *You, you usually very serious, competent, type-A person, stick to the plan. Get it together.*

So, how did I find my donor in the end? He turned out to be one of my best friends from college. Someone I had been keeping apprised of my plan as I went along, mostly because he was not on the official list. He was in a long-term relationship when I made my list. Though, in truth, he was on the highly classified, secret list, the one in the back of my brain, that I didn't even let my conscious-self look at. That list was so secret I didn't even know who else was on it. Maybe it was only him? He lived in San Francisco, and I was in town to attend meetings related to a work assignment. We were hanging out on the weekend. His girlfriend had recently moved out and we were catching up on how that was going. We met up at a hipster gardening shop that had its own barista. He was picking out plants and checking out wooly pocket systems for a living wall he was contemplating as a symbolic new beginning at life. It was a cool sunny San Francisco day in the gentrified part of Potrero Hill. We were sitting on a powdered coated metal bench shaded by giant fennel growing out of terra cotta pots and he asked the question himself. Would I want him as my donor? Like a stalk of the most tender, promisingly green, young asparagus, the idea popped open between us. The most natural thing in the world.

Homemade Baby of Your Dreams

ECONOMICALLY SPEAKING, becoming a single parent made me nervous. I needed to channel a new level of thrift—take shortcuts and start saving my loose change immediately. And this started with avoiding a costly fertility clinic, if I could.

While growing up, the two critical messages a Chinese girl receives regularly are: Earn money and don't get pregnant. The first part is explicit. It encompasses life choices such as working hard at school, pursuing only white-collar occupations, and marrying a person successful at making money. The second part gets communicated more implicitly because nobody thinks their daughters are having sex. Implicit but effective was that messaging, given that unplanned pregnancy was my biggest fear in high school. That's funny, because it was a completely theoretical risk. Back then, I had not ever been on a date. But it was the biggest fear because it promised a nosedive in my life potential; a future of hardship and financial struggle.

When my sister and I were little and there was a situation in which we wanted things, toys like our friends had, or trendy things to wear, my father often would say in a deep, but teasing voice, "What?!? Do you think you're a princess or something?" And mostly he said it as a joke, but it did what it was designed to do: develop consciousness about money and how much things cost and who was working hard to pay for it. It had its intended effect of cultivating in me a reluctance to ask for things from my parents. That is perfect Chinese parenting. Raising your kids in a way that they never ask for anything, but that you are able to give them everything that will help them to attain wealth and success. In all ways, we had it pretty easy growing up, we were sheltered and given many opportunities, and underlying this privilege was an expectation that we would be productive and self-sufficient upon leaving college and eventually have adequate resources and filial piety to take care of our parents when that became necessary.

The path toward wealth was best taken slowly and methodically. Work hard, earn money, save money, spend minimally, invest in real estate, save more money. The Chinese have long adopted the concept of reduce, reuse, recycle but more as an economic strategy rather than an effort towards environmental sustainability. I remember watching my grandmother cutting four-ply napkins in half because if you were brought up correctly, needing more than a two-ply napkin to eat tidily was excessive. Once when we visited the mainland, my aunt took my family out to a steakhouse. We were encouraged to fill up on the all-you-could-eat salad bar and have most of our steaks wrapped to take home to be eaten for lunch the next day. On the way home, we sat in the car, holding doggie bags on our laps as if they were trophies. From a young age, I was like the Pake Police in my family. (Pake is a pidgin term we used when growing up for being a stingy (typically Chinese) person.) Once in fifth grade, while waiting with my older sister at a bus stop, I chastised her for being too free-wheeling with her quarters when she said she was going to use a pay-phone to call our parents to ask if they could come pick us up, "Just be patient! Don't waste the quarter! Mom and Dad would be so disappointed in you!" She rolled her eyes at me and picked up the handset to dial.

Given my upbringing and having made it through my twenties and mid-thirties fiscally responsible and childless, naturally, my first effort to make a donor baby would be a low-cost, homemade one.

Insurance companies barely pay for treatments of couples proven to be infertile. My insurance company required medical documentation that a couple had been trying to conceive for at least a year before it would pay for infertility treatments. And even with said documentation, they paid for only one round of IVF. After that, it was all paying out of pocket. I guessed that my policy probably did not cover people who were not legally married or people trying with multiple different partners over the course of a year. I never confirmed it with my insurance company, but I was pretty sure the policy did not provide options for people who were not in a partnership and had no means of trying.

It's kind of an interesting question: is being able to have a child fundamental to health and well-being, the way (at the moment) contraception for not having a child is now part of a basic package of health services? Or maybe another stark comparison: is being able to have an erection more fundamental to well-being than being able to have a child? So, if you need drugs or a medical procedure in order to have a child, shouldn't your insurance company be obligated to pay for it? And if insurance begins paying for infertility treatment for people in heterosexual couples, don't they also have to pay for the same procedure for gay couples or people who aren't in a partnership? That is as far as my musing went. I did not have time to be Loo vs. the Hawai'i Medical Service Association Insurance Company test of jurisprudence, my biological clock was ticking.

So, now that I had a willing donor, I just had to figure out how to get pregnant. In my youth, sex was the cheapest way to make the most costly mistake of my life. But now twenty years later, trying to figure out a way to have a baby on my own, the thrift of unprotected casual sex as a method of baby making seemed a beautiful thing.

I was close friends with my donor, but I still saw the importance of maintaining some—what is the right term?—professional relationship, but that's not quite the way to say it. I was looking for a way to be clear about exactly what I was doing with my donor. My donor was not my partner, he was a supporter. So, while I wanted a cheap way to make a baby, I wanted the process to follow certain rules and procedures. To be very deliberate and measured. I wanted it to feel like baking a very elaborate cake, rather than throwing together an omelet from whatever's in the fridge the morning after a drunken hook up. I wanted a homemade baby, but not a naturally conceived one.

Plotting the home-made baby period was one of those times in my life that has underscored the advantages of being born at the right time and the right place. Socially and technologically, making a baby this way was unusual but within the realm of acceptable and possible. Most importantly, thank goodness for the internet. Advances in fertility medicine notwithstanding, the internet had a most powerful impact on these proceedings. What an optimistic commentary on society that just as there are online resources for making a bomb in your home, so too are there resources for making babies.

In this spirit, my thanks go out to a contingent of lesbian women in the blogosphere. Most of the information through my internet "research" I found was based on the very practical and explicit experience of lesbian couples trying to conceive cheaply through the collusion of their male friends or family members. There was a lot of information out there. Technical, legal, financial, testimonial, emotional. There were timelines, results of product testing, troubleshooting, and words of encouragement. There were postings by all kinds of women: sarcastic women and saccharine women, one-with-Mother-Nature women, down-to-earth women, and just giving the facts, ma'am kinds of women.

At first, I wondered why there was not not more information from gay men. Surely, they were trying to conceive children too. I thought maybe lesbians are less able to afford professional fertility treatments than gay men. Or that the kinds of gay men who wanted kids were more likely to be able to afford surrogacy and fertility clinics. Or maybe, and more likely, gay men in this situation preferred not to blog in great technical detail about such personal travails. In the end, I recognize that home insemination more often than not connotes the absence of men on the scene. So, what could men write about, not being actual witnesses or active parties in these acts of insemination? I still think that even if they were there, baby making, no matter how it's done, is a subject for the kind of blog women write, not men.

The homemade baby method is most often referred to in shorthand as the turkey baster method. That tickles me, because making a homemade baby the way I was planning to has definite parallels to preparing a holiday feast to be served up for the scrutiny of your extended family. (More on that later.) There will be overt and behind-your-back critique about how things are done. Some members of the family will give you unsolicited advice. Many prefer a traditional method; others are more open to Turducken or spatchcocking the bird and want to know in excruciating detail everything you went through. Did you brine it? Is there a glaze? What's in the stuffing? How heavy? How long? How hot? The fertility clinic route was like plucking a turkey trussed and stuffed with a duck stuffed with a chicken stuffed with Andouille sausage and chestnuts from the refrigerated case at a fancy butcher. Homemade baby was definitely more akin to grilling the turkey perched over an open can of beer in my garage.

After some amount of study of the logistics of home insemination, the biggest challenge appeared to be transport. My donor was in San Francisco. I was in Hawai'i. Correction, I was in Hawai'i maybe only 70% of the time. That was a non-trivial detail for scheduling the transport of live goods. I needed reliable transport from San Francisco to Hilo (or wherever in the US I was). This involved special coolers and cold packs that did not need dry ice, and that were accepted by FedEx. It involved special vials prefilled with media to stabilize the sperm during their journey. And large-sized plastic syringes that would get the sperm from the vial into my uterus. Okay, the syringe was not an issue related to transport, but I want to assure people that the turkey baster method is a misnomer and, thanks to medical equipment available through internet shopping, the lowly kitchen baster has been replaced by a more appropriate, hygienic technology. (This off-topic remark also serves the purpose of assuring people who were invited to my house for dinner and who ate poultry between June and December 2011, should not have had nor ever have reason to feel squeamish.)

The blogs I read spelled out the details of the equipment I needed and offered links to how to buy things in kits. So, I bought the kits. They cost several hundred dollars, but I got a discount for buying three at a time. There were delivered to San Francisco and my donor kept them in his bachelor-style refrigerator next to the sparkling water, bottle of sriracha, and single serve packets of butter and cream collected from packages of take-out.

Insemination kits on hand, I was ready to whip up Batch One of Homemade Baby. I let myself schedule work trips for the beginning and end of my cycle, leaving a good 14-day period in between when it was most likely for me to be at my fertile peak. Then the weeks I was working from home, I did what other normal women trying to get pregnant do. I peed on a stick in the morning and guessed whether ovulation was happening. But when my luteinizing hormone levels spiked, I did not schedule some sex with my partner. Instead, I had to text my donor and he would schedule himself to get home and produce some stuff and get it in the cooler box and off to a FedEx for next day 3 PM delivery to Honolulu. And since I lived in Hilo, the next day I would fly myself to Honolulu in the late morning. Because it seemed more predictable for me to meet FedEx in Honolulu, than to rely on another leg of transporting time sensitive goods from Honolulu to Hilo. For me, it was a low stress, one-hour flight. I would spend the early afternoon prowling around my parents' home waiting for the delivery. Tracking the package's progress from San Francisco to Honolulu; from dock to truck to door.

It felt anticlimactic to receive the package from the FedEx guy. He had no idea he was such a critical link in this process of impregnation. He had no idea he was participating in the miracle of creating life, his actions part of a symbolic, 2500-mile-long medical syringe connecting donor to uterus. How would he feel about that?

Maybe it is something similar to delivering a box of live chicks which have traveled across the country. He'd probably done that before. After hearing the little peeps coming from the air holes, I'm sure he took extra care not to turn the box upside down, or jostle it too much. My package was clearly a laboratory specimen of some kind. What if he could hear the spermatozoa sloshing around in their vial? Would he treat them gingerly, wish them *bon chance*? Would he be disturbed that he was delivering it to a regular residence, not a sterile laboratory? Would he be judging me, my desire, my process?

Or was he just "trying to do my job, Lady," so it didn't matter if the package contained live animals, or heirloom tomato seeds or somebody's cum, as long as he got it to where it was supposed to go on time. Maybe he really would not care. His blank expression while I nervously signed for the package was perhaps the most professional interaction involved with this endeavor so far.

Once I had the cooler, I took it to an upstairs bathroom. According to the printed instructions for optimizing fertilization which I had downloaded from my online source, in the bathroom I had already assembled a set of yoga blocks and, as recommended by these instructions, some porn, or at least the closest thing to porn that was available in my parents' home, a copy of Nicholson Baker's *Vox*. According to the New Yorker review, it is a *"phone-sex novel so steamy that Monica Lewinsky gave it as a gift to Bill Clinton."* I had bought it at a used bookstore a couple of years ago, while visiting my parents, but had never read it. It was a novel that had come out the year I graduated from high school, and I remember some boy in my class had kind of gone off about it and all the sex. Phone sex. It meant something different today, than it did in 1992, but it seemed appropriate for the style of impregnation I was engaged in.

Clearly, this was not a high tech, well-outfitted insemination facility. Later I would learn that fancy clinics have dedicated rooms for sperm production, i.e. jack-off rooms, with porn for all tastes and sexual preferences, dim lighting, and facilities for music, possibly sound proofing for the comfort of everyone. Whatever is needed to get the goods. That was not this. The mantra of home-made baby was *Do-the-best-you-can-with-what-you-got*.

There were about to be some minor acrobatics going on in that bathroom. I set myself up lying on the floor perpendicular to the tub, my hips elevated with the yoga blocks into a quasi-supported bridge pose, my feet resting on the edge of the tub. I had assembled the syringe, opened the vial, and began breathing deeply. It was tricky, drawing the sample into the plastic syringe, maneuvering the 8-inch-long flexible tip from vial to human receptacle, then depressing the plunger without spilling or leaking everywhere. It is not easy to do when you are half upside-down, but trying to hold a vial upright. You cannot see that well, and you are working against gravity. And semen, in case you didn't know, is not a normal liquid, it has weird surface tension. It is alive and generally non-cooperative. And in the vial, it was suspended in the media to help it survive transport. It was the texture of egg whites, unbeaten. Preferring to slide around in clumps rather than one smooth homogenous liquid.

Somehow, I inseminated myself. But it wasn't all over. The page I had printed out from the internet recommended that one masturbate, so that you're well lubricated, making a welcoming environment for the sperm. And then stay with your hips elevated for at least 20 minutes. Staying elevated I could do. But this was not my idea of a sexy activity. I was not really in the mood to masturbate. I was on the floor of a bathroom in my parents' home. They had seen me receive the package and go upstairs. They kind of had a vague notion of what was going on. At the macro-level only, I hoped. For their own sake I hope they were not thinking it through too much. It was worrisome, but I decided I couldn't really be responsible for everybody's feelings.

Meanwhile, my neck had a crick in it. But I was trying to create a maximally welcoming environment for the frat party going on in my uterus, so I took out Vox and began to read, trying to get a bit inspired. It was a bad book. Not entertaining. It did not get me in the mood. I was feeling annoyed. As described in Wikipedia, "*For some readers, Baker's obsession with detail detracted from a hoped-for pornographic effect.*" Yeah, that about sums it up. But I dutifully stayed there, perched with my hips on those blocks, for at least 20 minutes, the blood pooling in my head, and hopefully the sperm swimming, swimming their hardest, or at least given my uteral topography, draining into position, ready to be in the right place at the right time. I only hoped that my eggs were with the program and the ovulation predictor was right and this whole endeavor wasn't some incredible waste of time. I was raised to hate waste, remember: reduce, reuse, recycle. The best approach was to do something the minimal number of times possible, using the least amount of resources. I was honoring that tradition, if not any other Chinese tradition related to my filial duty to produce grandchildren.

Two weeks later, I tested myself and figured out it did not take. I tried again two months later. I happened to be in New Jersey visiting my sister. Her 9-year-old and 4-year-old were playing outside when the FedEx guy finally came. He was late. It was supposed to arrive the day before in the afternoon, but here it was 36 hours after they were put in the vial. I was frantic, my ovulation window was probably over, it was definitely not optimally peaked. The kids were yelling from the front yard, "Aunty, Aunty, you got a package."

"Don't touch it," I called out cheerfully, but firmly. "I'm coming." I did not want to scare them, but I did not want them handling that package. Bouncing it around, tapping the sides. I could see the sperm in their vial feeling as stressed as guppies coming home from the pet store in a plastic bag. I was worried that being subjected to my nephews' handling would be the last straw the sperm could take. The survivors might give up, just as they reached the literal and figurative doorstep.

I also was not sure the children should be exposed to this kind of thing. The less they had to do with it, the better.

And the easier. My sister probably would not appreciate the follow-up questions that might come. They were innocent. Sperm in the mail seemed so sordid. Explaining to the kids what was happening when I had my baby bump was a whole other issue that I would have to figure out. But answering the question, "oooh, what's in the box?" I was not sure what to say. I do not like lying to kids. But I had not prepared a thoughtful euphemism to describe what I was up to at that time. It was not technically some type of medicine, or just something I had ordered online. It was a gift, but the kind of gift I should open in a bathroom behind a locked door, and then quickly dispose of the rest of the contents of the box.

I grabbed the box and charged upstairs to the family bathroom. I needed to hustle to get the tired, weak, and dying sperm into my body. I did not have yoga blocks, I did not have porn, the conditions were already poor. I was not sure it was going to be worth the effort. Can you think of anything more depressing than lying on the floor of a bathroom shared with four other people, injecting yourself with someone else's body fluids when you suspect the stuff has already lost its potency? But the package was there and I had already called FedEx the day before, demanding a refund for the late delivery.

(I had put on quite a performance over the phone. Tearfully, I explained to the customer service representative how my "very important biological samples," had not arrived when promised. Through the break in my voice, I was trying to convey that the loss was heavy. I was nonspecific about what kind of medical specimens I had been expecting, to avoid judgment and protect my privacy. I hoped that the tone of my voice implied that there were human organs in the package. The representative could probably tell my address was not a medical facility and she probably knew that you do not send organs FedEx next day delivery. True, my package did not actually contain human organs, but how could she be sure? Since that tactic had not incurred sympathy, I then made sure she knew that now *everything*, in vague but monumental terms, was *ruined* due to the late delivery. And did I mention that I was devastated. She was still not sympathetic. So, I tried again to communicate what I was feeling the best that I could without mentioning my plight to have a child or have for myself what most other women had. Really, my end game was that I wanted her to refund the money for breach of contract and be so moved that she comped the next three deliveries. I misplayed my hand, I shifted to the moral high ground. She countered, offering contrition rather than credit. I hung up the phone).

Not surprisingly, the result of Batch Two was *nada, no embarazada*. So I did it again. In Honolulu, same set up as the first time, just different pornography. And the process got old very quickly. This part was not described in the blogs I read. It was a biased sample. People who posted the directions for basting home turkeys are the ones that ended up with babies. My donor's refrigerator was emptied of kits. His enthusiasm for this process waned. He found it hard to explain the contents of his ice box to people visiting his home. I was not that excited to invest in more kits either. The cost in effort and time was adding up and it was not yielding results. It just felt like waste.

I decided it was time to scrap the home-made baby plan and go to the professionals. I felt a bit defeated—almost embarrassed. I felt like I brined my turkey overnight in exotic spices, basted the bird all morning, and then realized my oven was not working. So, if I was going to feed all these people who were expecting to eat, much as I was reluctant to head to Boston Market and shell out for their traditional turkey meal with all the sides, I knew I had to do it. I told myself to get over it and embrace the idea of having to go to a clinic, because the purpose of all the effort was to have an enjoyable family meal, not to impress people that I cooked it in a particular way.

Picking a fertility clinic turned out to be a bit like online dating. (*Why* was almost every part of this process so far, a bit like online dating?) But this time I was looking for the fertility clinic equivalent of casual sex. I decided to work with a clinic in San Francisco, rather than Honolulu. There were many reasons for this. One of the reasons I decided against a clinic in Honolulu was because I needed to arrange for freezing donor sperm to be used over the course of multiple cycles. And I had read about the limited capability to store frozen reproduction products in the state. There was one story about a doctor who maintained one of the few facilities in his office, but had gotten diagnosed with a late-stage cancer and stopped practicing unexpectedly. That was a personal tragedy for sure, but it also left a lot of fertility patients in the lurch, with no access to the freezer or their goods and no way to contact the doctor. The situation had been resolved sometime later, when someone had been able to get in contact with the doctor and understand the circumstances of his hiatus. It was clear that San Francisco was probably a much more established infrastructure for making babies in clinics.

And then the other reason is because Hawaiʻi is a small place, everybody knows everybody and everybody feels comfortable getting into each other's business. When I had some paperwork for the fertility clinic notarized at my local bank, the bank teller noticed the topic of the contract and started telling me her own story of infertility and trying to have a baby with her second husband, who wasn't her husband at the time. She had her stamp poised over the paper and she asked me how my own process was going, how long had it taken to get to this stage. Some places this would be inappropriate, but here it was not unexpected. I gave her some cheerful line in exchange for her stamp and signature. Because in Hawai'i that's what you do. Smile and say something nice, no piss off da lady holding yo peh-pahs.

I called a couple of places in San Francisco and on the basis of location in the city and efficiency of the receptionist, I went with my gut and signed myself up with one of them. The one I liked had a good website and was located next to a Trader Joe's. Which I intended to hit after my appointments and stock up on cheap nuts, dried fruit, and snack foods to take back to Hawai'i. Yes, there were government compiled statistics on clinic success rates and online reviews of the clinics and individual doctors I could have used to guide my selection process. But I had the idea that this information did not really apply to me. I had no reason to think I had a fertility issue, and a majority of people going to fertility clinics have an infertility problem, so success rates are more applicable to those kinds of clients. And because I felt my procedures were elective and I was not stressed about infertility I thought the patient-doctor interface was not so important. I did not want to read the philosophy of the doctors at the clinic. I did not need to know which doctors patients preferred. I wasn't looking for the doctor who was most supportive when the first three treatments did not meet with success. I was looking for something slightly different than the average client reviewer. Because I was going to be flying to San Francisco to do this, I wanted a competent, efficient operation that had a flexible schedule and was not going to get into my personal business. I just wanted a clinic that could provide basic good quality insemination services.

There are advantages to doing what I was doing in California. It seems that the legal process of using a known sperm donor is well developed, due to the number of gay couples with an array of non-conventional arrangements that have been considered. A good clinic that works with a "known sperm donor" arrangement will not start any procedures until a legal agreement between the donor and the recipient is in place and the clinic has a copy on file. They often require a psychological evaluation for both parties as well; they try to cover everyone's bases. The last thing the clinic wants are people that are pre-dispositioned to be emotionally unstable hanging out in their waiting rooms, and walking through their halls or engaging them in lawsuits.

And so the first thing my donor and I had to do to become part of this elite group of private infertility clinic goers was to get lawyers. Separate lawyers and the kind who do this kind of thing a lot. The kind with boilerplates for baby makers. In truth, the legal agreement is a good idea, it spells out the intended relationship the donor has to your child, should the process be successful. It makes you say out loud to the other person and a witness, whether you want total authority over decision making for your child, and in what circumstances if any at all you would cede any bit of that authority. It even makes clear the relationship of your child to the donor's parents. It makes you say all those things explicitly to each other and makes you put your initials on every page of that document before you sign your full name to the line on the last page.

I think that is strange. Because before you conceive a child through sex, whether with a legal spouse, or a partner, or in a one-night stand, you do not say all those things. You do not make detailed statements about your intentions. It's not spoken, your expectation of taking full responsibility for another human, your expectation to have complete control until the age of majority or point of emancipation.

The other thing is that when I read over the contract the first time, I was surprised by the language of my very legal document. It uses the language of intention and ambition and aspiration. It says on the very first page, in the opening paragraph, that my donor's sole intention in providing his sperm was to "help me fulfill my hopes and dreams of having a child."

Hopes and dreams. I read it and thought to myself, *I never said that to myself before, I would never describe it to myself that way.* Calling it a hope or a dream made it sound like a faraway and unlikely event. It sounded like something that was a long shot and required a large measure of luck.

And it hit me then that I had not been so straight with myself. This *could* take a long time. This *might* be an unlikely event.

I had put myself in a different category than the other people using a fertility clinic. I had not wanted to make myself a statistic. By force of will, I believed the probability of my having a baby was 100%. I did not want to admit that I might need more than a professionally inserted syringe and some booster hormones from these people. I had not let myself think about what I would do, or how I would feel if this did not work.

THE PROFESSIONALS

THE MOST BASIC, NONINVASIVE, low-cost version of professional baby making is intrauterine insemination, or IUI as referenced in the literature provided by the clinic. The cost was moderate, only $600-700 a shot. What was different than the previously described edge-of-the-bathtub-hips-on-a-yoga-block method was that when done in a clinic, the "donor specimen" gets tested for diseases and washed before being applied to my uterus by a person with a specialized medical degree.

That description somewhat understates the total difference of the experience between homemade and clinic-based insemination.

First, it is useful to compare the human resources involved in each process. Instead of me, my donor, and the FedEx guy; my clinic experience was initiated through the assignment of a personal cycle coordinator. The cycle coordinator exists only to shepherd her client safely through the entire process: from receptionist, to psychologist, to billing agent, to doctor, to laboratorian, and back again, and around, and through, as needed. The coordinator has no authority, only information and a well-modulated tone of voice. My guide in this journey to realize my hopes and dreams was Bernadette.

In my mind, I referred to her as Bernadette, my beautiful launderette. I thought it was funny, until I saw the movie and realized that a launderette is a place to do one's laundry, not a French laundresse wearing a flirty outfit. And then it was just a sad metaphor for the clinic and its role as a glorified sperm washing facility.

My first encounter with Bernadette was by phone. Which was appropriate, given her characteristic, apologetic-by-nature tone of voice. She spoke gently, slowly and carefully as if she had an intense phobia of misunderstanding. Her speaking style was probably honed from years of delivering disappointing news to women—women in high stress situations who were being given information involving schedules and instructions to inject themselves with various substances while under either a natural or artificially induced heightened hormonal state. Women who had high expectations, sure that if they followed the instructions they were being given, if they trusted in the information their cycle coordinators were imparting, if they threw enough money at the problem, that they were likely to get the thing that they most desired in the world.

I suspected Bernadette's tone was part of an overall fertility clinic strategy to start with low expectations. I suspected she had been given personal defense training to protect herself from irate and distraught women until building security could arrive on the scene. I imagined she also received training similar to that given to zoo keepers and circus performers, people working with dangerous mammals: lions, elephants, gorillas and the like.

So it was on the phone that Bernadette first explained the process to me, the steps I would need to complete before I could initiate my first IUI cycle. Starting with the physical exam, the blood work needed, meeting with their psychologist. Then I explained to her that I was not living in San Francisco. There was a pause on Bernadette's side.

"Oh, I see."

She was probably reviewing her script, deciding if she needed to amend anything she had just told me. No, she decided, it was basically the same, so she continued.

As if it wasn't obvious to me, she said, "You will need to come to the clinic at specific times during the selected cycle in order to complete all the steps." She paused to see if that was a surprise. Maybe I hadn't understood that the physical limitations of my cycle needed to be taken into account, Bernadette was just confirming.

"Though," she offered as consolation to my lack of control over my fertility outcomes, "it is totally your choice on how much time before the IUI procedure you would want to come up to San Francisco...unless...you are planning to stay in the area for the whole cycle?"

"No, I was planning to spend most of the time at home and come up to San Francisco for the necessary appointments." I heard Bernadette make a handwritten note. I noticed that she began to speak even more slowly. Maybe that was part of the training—slowing down when the cycle coordinator assesses she has to be even more careful about expectations given the greater improbability of the desired outcome.

And then I told her I was using a known donor. "Ahhh." She issued an oral indicator that the script needed to be rewound a bit and reviewed. Large pause. This information did add a few steps to the process. There were a few more questions. Where was the donor located? Were we in a relationship? How was he planning to provide the specimens? Did I know about the FDA testing requirements that were necessary for the clinic to be able to accept the specimens? She reviewed the costs associated with using a known donor. There were things I needed to do. And things the donor needed to do. And things I needed to do after the donor completed the things he needed to do. By this time, Bernadette was speaking very slowly. The cultivated control of her voice did something to me.

I did feel like a wild animal. I wanted to jump up and down and pound my chest, "Just tell me how I'm going to get my baby!"

And then after that, she circled back to the question I had asked at the beginning of the conversation, "Is it likely that I can start the process during my current cycle?"

"Ummm (large pause) it would be (large pause) difficult (apologetic in tone). But, (shift in tone toward optimism) it might be possible. Though (large pause), it would be very difficult (thoughtful pause). Very difficult (apologetic pause)."

Maybe Bernadette was trained never to give a firm no. Fertility clinics communicate in the language of probability. Better never to give a firm yes, and likewise, no need to ever say no. "But to help things along," Bernadette suggested, "why don't you give me your donor's contact information so I can review the process with him. I can get him the information he needs."

I gave her what she wanted. I hung up the phone. And then I called my donor to warn him that Bernadette would be calling. There were things we needed to do and it was going to require some more time and effort. But if he was game for it, I figured he could put some sperm in the bank and then be done for a while. The rest would be up to me and the fine professionals at the fertility center.

From the elevator bank on the fifth floor, only the letters "[X] FC" were on the sign board. It could have been a real estate firm or an accountant's office that the clients were going to. But it was the [X] Fertility Center. Inside, the office continued its warm gray tones. The wall behind the reception resembled highly magnified dead white coral, undulating with sculpted grooves. The walls looked womanly in a slightly sterile way. The reception counter itself was high. Probably to hide the files of barren couples and the mundane office supplies and to project to clients only that this was a highly efficient place of business.

The women behind the counter wore asymmetrical origami folded blouses or natural colored wool cowl-necked sweaters. Subtle shades of off-neutral lip color, no gloss. They spoke in hushed, sensitive-tones which maintained the line of professionalism but hinted at the well of sympathy beneath their well-tailored tops. They all looked too young to be thinking about having children, young and beautiful without a fertility care in the world.

(The cycle coordinators, on the other hand, had a more wrinkled presentation both in skin and dress. They probably had had their kids, and with that experience could lead each of their clients over the hump of infertility into the doldrums of sleeplessly raising children and commuting from Colma or Portola.)

The waiting room featured a set of plush banquettes in tasteful modern jacquard: abstract circular shapes woven into the fabric in subtle blues, grays, with accents of indigo. There were upholstered stackable arm chairs lining the inner oval of chairs facing the banquettes. The beverage center featured a carafe of hot water, an array of silken non-caffeinated tea bags, hot chocolate mix, and wooden stirrers. Large boxes of moisture doux tissues were placed around the room. The magazine table offered *Self*, *Yoga Journal*, and *Simply Organized*. Nothing with women under 40 on the cover, no populist news magazines, no implications that settling down and becoming a homemaker ten years ago would have helped to avoid the need to sit in this waiting room.

The first few visits to [X] FC, I alternated between feeling superior and a bit like a voyeur while waiting for my appointment. The other patients came in looking somber, older, and much better put together than me. People scanned the room quickly to see who they might run into, picked a corner that helped them to avoid eye contact with someone else waiting. Some took out files from their oversized leather tote bags and started reading, careful to respect the "no cell-phone" tent cards distributed around the room.

There was an air of stress, a tinge of panic in the waiting room. I felt like a woman coming in for Botox, while the rest had been scheduled for chemotherapy. I was coming to the clinic, electing to get pregnant, they were coming to treat their infertility. I thought to myself, *They should have a separate waiting room for people like me.*

Let's get to the cycle. I fly into SFO on Day 12. Day 13, I go to the clinic for my ultrasound. From where I'm staying, I call a taxi, take an $18 ride and get dropped off at the corner. I pull open the smoky gray, double glass doors. I nod to the building security guard, then take the elevator to the 5th floor, and I enter the clinic. I check in with reception. She invites me to have a seat while I wait for Bernadette. I choose the couch with the view of Alcatraz on a clear day. Another woman is already waiting. Her cycle coordinator comes out and sits next to her. Cycle coordinators do not get offices to meet with their clients. They have a whispered conversation on another couch, their legs pressed neatly together, hands on their lap. Sometimes the coordinator touches her client's shoulder. This is part of the personal touch. Bernadette emerges. She sits next to me. She softly inquires how I am doing. She gives me an encouraging smile and then leaves. I think her role today is supposed to be only ceremonial.

A nurse comes to fetch me to a room, before I get too deeply into the latest issue of *Self* magazine. Oddly, it is never the same nurse, even when I come in multiple times for the same cycle. They all seem to be learning the ropes, they often have to leave the room to retrieve a chart or ask a question before they can advise me. They always seem half apologetic that I have to be there. Maybe it's because they have to talk to me while I sit there without my pants, a wrap of mauve colored crepe paper providing minimal dignity. The nurse wears dumpy scrubs, so I feel sorry for her too. Neither of us is dressed in our best. My socks lie in disarray on the floor, but my pants are folded nicely and hung over the side of a chair. If she looked closely, she would see my underwear tucked in neatly like a pocket square. I arranged them that way to signal I could hang with the private fertility clinic crowd. I was brought up well and went to the kind of school where people know where to put their underwear when they go to the doctor's office.

"The doctor (she meant Dr. Will) will come in soon," the nurse says and leaves me alone. Usually, it takes between 15 or 20 minutes for Will to actually arrive. I sit there debating whether I should get up and retrieve the magazine I brought with me, which is in the bag on the chair near the door with my pants. The dilemma was whether Will would come in at that exact moment I got up and go to get the magazine, and I would expose myself to Will and the rest of the nursing staff in the hallway. It is the same awful decision about whether to start walking to your destination which takes half an hour to walk, or to wait for the bus, because as soon as you get halfway in between stops the bus will roar past you. But if you wait for the bus, it will take another 15 or 20 minutes to get there.

But let me tell you, it is best to sit and wait for Will. Will is the bus worth waiting for. Eventually, he floats in, all pleasant. He is not quite like a breath of fresh air, he is more like a cumulonimbus cloud, mostly because he is a man without color. His slightly wavy hair is pale gray, his skin is beige, he has thin colorless lips, and wears a white coat. This alone gives him the look of a sad specter. I wonder if he really is sad, and if it is because he must see women all day, mostly at their craziest and loneliest. And he knows these are women who can pay for things, but can't buy the thing they want most, only pay for the chance to try to get it. And all day he must come in the room feeling hopeful, and greet them cheerfully, and all day he sticks his magic wand inside them and tries to tell them in a positive way how big their follicles are and how thick their linings are, all the while, knowing they are not quite big enough or thick enough and though he wishes them the best of luck, they are really just shooting in the dark.

And while the women are staring at the screen that shows them what Will sees, he can interpret the pictures so they can see the future and all the hope that is growing within them. Today is just my ultrasound day, it's not the day he squirts my specimen deep inside my uterus, that is tomorrow or the day after. Today we are just doing a look-see. And I know the drill, keep peeing on the stick until my o.p. (ovulation predictor) kit turns positive. And if it's not positive in two days, to call for next steps. Will gives me a brave smile and says, "See you in a few days!" And then he floats out leaving me to put on my pants and go for billing.

The billing people are set up just in front of the exit. There is a whole flank of them, so you never have to wait to give your credit card to them. And then before I sign the receipt, a nurse (different one) runs up behind me because they forgot to give me my calendar, which basically is a print out of all the days of the month and in tomorrow's box it says "o.p. kit" and in the box for the day after tomorrow it says "o.p. kit" and then after that "call office." She wants to make sure I have this important document that helps to make the schedule of events less complicated.

As if, after calling in on Day 1 and taking drugs Day 3-7 and peeing on a stick first thing in the morning since Day 10, and hopping on a plane on Day 12, and coming for an ultrasound on Day 13, and ordering my injectable ovulation stimulator to arrive on the same day, that I won't be able to remember that I have to keep peeing on a stick for two more days, and will have to be reminded to call. As if, if I didn't have the reminder, I would sit in my hotel for another three or four days, just continuing to pee on a stick. The nurse begins to look sad. Maybe she was sorry I had to be there listening to her talk. And sorry that she would probably never see me again.

On my way out of the building, I am facing toward Embarcadero and the pier that takes the tourist to Alcatraz Island. It is busy and always seems a nice day for a boat ride, but I turn the other direction and walk the grid toward downtown. Coit Tower is on the cliff just above, and I find it comforting to have such a large hopeful penis symbol to my right. On my left is the lonely but lovely isle of Alcatraz, representing my uterus, surrounded by shark infested waters which symbolizes my lack of sex life, much less life partner. And that to my back is the [X] FC that is going to help me bridge this gulf in between. Ahead of me lies a quintessential Bay Area bakery which makes fancy sandwiches with house charcuterie. This is my immediate future, just a few blocks away at the Ferry Building. Soon I will be sitting on a bench, eating from waxy paper, letting the artisanal pickle juice drip down my chin as the gulls swoop around the deck looking toward the grand Bay Bridge. While I eat my sandwich, I think positive thoughts.

If it goes as planned, on Day 14, I get a positive pee stick test, and then that afternoon I inject my tummy with a last bit of ovulation stimulator that launches my follicles from their tubes, on their way to meet Pale Prince Will's other magic wand. By evening, the surge in my belly is strong. It's like in Top Gun, when Tom Skerritt explains to Tom Cruise how his father died: *It was a dog fight with the Russians, Son, it was like fireflies in the sky.* That is what it is like in my fallopian tubes, like fireflies in the skies, except they are bogeys crashing around in there. It's a dogfight of ripe follicles, Tom, not marshmallows 'round a campfire!

The next morning, I go in for my insemination. But this time, the receptionist doesn't let me sit down, doesn't wait for Bernadette. She escorts me personally to Billing first thing, because my patient passport has the word "Prepay" stamped across the top in red ink. And so, I pay the $450 in advance. I wonder what experience they had that made the insistent "Prepay" protocol so important. Did they find people in such a daze after being inseminated or emotional and overwrought that they can't get it together to dig out their credit card. Or is it because they let me lie there on the table after it's all over, lights dimmed for however long I like, to make sure that the sperm has the best chance of commingling and infiltrating, splitting and implanting into that soft cushy lining of my uterus, that Will and I so carefully cultivated. And they don't want to break the mood by recognizing that this beautiful experience has to be paid for.

Whatever the reason, the [X] FC gets paid, the deed gets done,. The next day, I board the plane and go home.

And now the waiting begins. Two weeks of eating prenatal vitamins for dessert. Two weeks of tucking in a vaginal suppository every night before bed. I whisper sweet thoughts to it, making sure it's comfortable and snug in there, before closing my eyes. Remembering not to eat raw honey, remembering not to eat the soft cheese, indulge in mid-day spicy tuna maki at the supermarket. In yoga that week, I Marichyasana 3, a twist to squeeze the toxins out.

And I wonder, maybe I am squeezing my hard-fought egg and sperm combo. And so, I twist the other way and not so tightly and then I decide to Child's Pose for the rest of the session. The rest of the session until Savasana. And the whole time I am gently breathing and observing my abdomen and the twinges and thinking, just thinking, the thought continues to pass through, thinking about whether that is pregnancy, indigestion, or other types of cramping. Can you feel the thing implanting, or can you just feel the lining peeling away from the sides of your uterus? And that's how you know the production is a bust. You wake up with your period, your body striking down the set after a two week run. On to the next show, next cycle, back on the road.

CHANCES ARE

I HAD ALREADY COMPLETED IUI three times. None of which did the trick. My donor had been called to replenish his initial deposit at the PFC. I imagined Bernadette sitting in her home office, maybe in a garret, near a window that had a very small part of the Golden Gate Bridge peeking through. She was looking through a binder with my name on the front, her hand poised on the receiver of an old spiral corded phone. And so I was not entirely surprised when my phone rang and it was Bernadette calling to talk to me about "Other Options."

She started with a carefully phrased recap of where I was in the process. And then with her slowly manipulative pregnant pausing, she got me to say, "IVF." And to confirm she heard what she thought she heard, she repeated, "in vitro fertilization?" And then after I had confirmed, she said very cheerfully, she could certainly connect me to an IVF coordinator, if I wanted to discuss that option. (Hopeful pause.) She could see the light at the end of her tunnel that was my journey toward impregnation.

It turned out that cycle coordinators were not authorized to go through the details of IVF. But I guessed cycle coordinators might get a bonus or a gold star for delivering a patient to the IVF department. "Great," I said. Pause. I agreed it was probably time to think about that as a next step.

I don't remember the name of my IVF coordinator. It was kind of a blur. She had more energy in her voice, or at least she spoke at a faster clip. This began to feel like we were building a rocket, rather than preparing methodically to go for a hot air balloon ride. She said she would mail me a binder of materials to review, and then let her know when would be a good time to do a call to talk through any questions I had. There was basic information about what IVF entailed, the options for stimulating follicle production, specific fertilization procedures, and of course the big unknown I was most interested in, the associated costs and payment plans available.

The latter took up a lot of pages. It needed a lot of fuel to make this rocket leave the ground, get past the atmosphere and deliver the payload. There were several options. Pay as you go. Monthly installments. And then there was one option that offered "IVF insurance." In that option, you paid more up front, but if the IVF round did not result in implantation, then you got a certain percentage of the fee back. If you did get your baby, you've just spent more to get that baby. What's another couple of thousand dollars? At that point, you don't care.

Infertility insurance sounded like something I should think about more deeply. It was appealing in moments of uncertainty, when I wasn't clear investing so much money into conceiving was a wise decision. But on the other hand, it felt too much like hedging my bets. Betting against my hopes and dreams. It's like saying to yourself that if this rocket ship crashes, you could still hobble away from the devastation. But what do you do with your refund? "You could potentially reinvest that money into another round of IVF," the IVF coordinator suggested.

Or, I thought to myself, I could invest in some other concrete part of my life: make a down payment on a car or use it to pay *down my mortgage.* But those things seemed trivial compared to "buying" a baby. I could invest in adoption, but that seemed expensive too. And did it transfer some bad juju to invest failed IVF money into another process for getting a kid? One already fraught with similar probabilities of not working out? Besides costing lots of money, adoption seemed to be a nail biting waiting game for babies to be available and big emotions with biological parents. I thought my chances of getting selected to adopt were pretty dicey. I was single. I was a consultant, and I traveled extensively for work. I could pledge to get a regular job, but I hadn't proved I could or would do it to create a stable environment to raise a child.

Before going down that rabbit hole, I really needed to figure out how to pay for IVF. To insure or not to insure? Was this not the perfect situation to apply my knowledge of statistics to make a decision? It didn't make sense to me that they offered the same insurance plan to everybody trying to do IVF. Insurance is supposed to be a highly calibrated empirically driven product. The clinic must have made some calculation based on their success rates to figure out how many people needed to buy insurance, so the extra money paid by people who were successful would offset the money paid out to people who failed. Why wouldn't an older woman using her own eggs and old man sperm pay more because she was more likely to fail?

Because that's not how this insurance scheme worked, it occurred to me that this was a scam. That somehow the odds were such that the house, i.e. [X] FC, was always going to win and probably win big. They must have the power to calculate a margin on the insurance plan such that they were safely making quite a bit of additional revenue off this scheme. I immediately dismissed any prior thought that [X] FC might offer insurance as an altruistic, stress lowering option for patients. On principle, I couldn't go for it. I didn't want to make monthly installments on a baby I couldn't afford either, so I went with "pay as you go." I would see how far my savings would get me.

What bothered me most about this process of trying to get pregnant—all the effort that went into upping the probability of it happening and the careful allocation of my resources: how many times to try the turkey baster method before going to IUI? How many times to try IUI before going to IVF? How many cycles to rest in-between? Did it matter if the sperm were frozen or fresh? Did it matter if I was on a long-haul flight, if I had a big deadline, or if I was in a bad mood during that cycle?

At the end of the day, for all the calculations and thinking and contortions to do the things that would make a difference, my analysis made clear that I really had no control over the whole situation.

Part of the problem was the way I was thinking about probability. The success rate for IVF in my age group at my clinic was 42%. Is that high? It's less than 50-50. So is that low? It was higher than the national average. That made me feel better. When I took statistics in grad school, my professor repeated again and again that the probability of the event happening to an individual is 0 or 1. What he meant was that probabilities don't apply to individuals. Statistics are about figuring out the proportion of people in a group of a particular makeup who are going to have some experience. It could be getting a disease, it could be having some physical feature, it could be experiencing an act of God. One kind of public health statistics is about calculating what happened to one group of people or things in the past and then trying to use that information to predict what might happen to another similar group in the future or to determine the plausibility of if what happened to the group occurred by chance. But too often, we try to apply statistics to predicting what will happen to ourselves or another person we know. That's not how statistics works. If there is a 0.1% probability of people like me getting breast cancer, I will either get breast cancer or not get breast cancer. I don't personally have a 0.1% chance in my life of getting breast cancer. And even though I belong to a group for which there is reliable data that measures the proportion of people who will get breast cancer in a group similar to mine, the chance of getting breast cancer is not the same for everyone in my group.

I knew that, but I still applied those statistics to my own personal situation when I made the decision to try IVF. I knew better and I still figured that my chances of getting a baby through this process was greater than 42%. There's nothing like the secret fear that despite your best efforts, significant resources, and faith in positive thinking that there was a faintly inscribed number in a corner of your uterus, written in by fate many years ago, and that number was zero.

Waging an unspoken war with a sense of futility was familiar to me as a consultant working in the development sector. For all the training and experience you might bring to a country you work with, your time is limited and by nature you cannot be a day-to-day presence to help troubleshoot and carry out the best-laid plans that comprise your work product. The country client has called you in to work on a problem, you meet with counterparts, do field visits and participate in planning sessions. You might leave a well articulated design and detailed action plan to meet their objective, but by the time they receive it you have probably left the country. Maybe you return periodically to do a training, visit implementation sites, or review data on the results, but success is not in your control and even your best efforts cannot guarantee a result.

Things happen on the ground, the players change and have different ideas or capacities, nobody knows where the last person kept the copy of the report that you produced. Funding runs out or competing needs emerge and suddenly nobody is getting paid to carry out the work. Sometimes the plan turns out not to make sense because you didn't involve the right people who really knew how things worked. So this group hired you to do your best and make things work, but it didn't—turns out they were taking their chances too. And nobody offered them insurance on their investment.

The stakes seemed high to me doing this baby-making work. And I suppose I should have been used to it, more comfortable with my decisions while working in transactional spaces with calculated risks and little encouragement. Why was I expecting this to be different? After all, stability and security are not reasons why people go into consulting. Your value is your work product; nobody is investing in you, but yourself. So it is easy to feel expendable when you work as a consultant. The organization that contracts you has no responsibility to your health or life outside of what impacts your ability to fulfill your contract. And generally, as a single working person, the people around you make assumptions about what you are willing to do and how available you may be to do the job. Chances are you can work late, travel more; chances are you are more flexible about giving up holidays, or take assignments with bigger security risks.

It's different when you have a family unit, dependents. Somehow, that makes you more substantial, more human. People tell you to take better care of yourself because someone depends on you. Don't ride the moto taxi, don't take a red eye, don't take evening meetings. You have to help put the kids to bed. You get a pass for being dead weight at an institution because you rely on the international benefits to pay for private school or college or health insurance for the whole family. When you're part of a unit, then you're less accepting about taking chances. You need guarantees or at least you prioritize things with greater certainty. You join an organization. And your organization puts their resources in making sure you're successful, because their fortunes are tied to yours.

It was December 22nd in 2008 or maybe 2009. My task team leader, Emanuele, an exuberant Italian prone to throwing up when he got stressed, and I were both scheduled to leave Kabul that afternoon. His wife and two year-old were already at their family home in the Italian Alps, ready to celebrate Christmas. I was just headed back home to Hawai'i. Nothing special planned. But then Hamidullah, the operations officer for the World Bank in Afghanistan radioed the guesthouse to inform us that our flight had been canceled.

At the time, World Bank security measures for missions to Afghanistan included issuing heavy radio handsets to each person upon arrival, to be carried on our person wherever we went. Other security measures included not walking more than five meters on the street when we were outside the World Bank compound. The armor plated SUVs were literally supposed to drive us door-to-door, including to cross the street from one secured building to another. At the time of Hamidullah's message, he knew we were all in the World Bank guest house, because it was his job to coordinate vehicle transport for everyone on mission in Kabul. He could have easily reached us through the house phone but I think he liked the idea of announcing our fates with the seriousness that radio communique entailed.

Our suitcases were already in the hallway of the World Bank guesthouse and we were having our last "American" breakfast of Alpen cereal, white toast, synthetic cheese and a pair of pale-yolked fried eggs. We were expected to finish the mission report before we left country. It was in the final stages of drafting, and over cereal we were debating the last recommendation and whether to make the next disbursement of funds contingent on its follow up. Highlights of the report would be presented to the Minister of Health just before lunch, and then we would be driven to the airport to catch the plane.

Hamidullah's voice crackling over the radio sobered my team leader. The mission report was tabled. Immediately, my team leader put in a call to Hamidullah. When was the next flight out, was there room on it? My team leader foresaw a chain of events involving calls to his wife, arrangements with the American Express travel agent to reroute the ongoing flight to Rome. We were on the cusp of the heaviest days of travel for the holidays. Rebooking was going to be ugly.

I had been so looking forward to getting out of Kabul. Afghanistan was the only place I worked where you had to pass through a metal detector to get into the Minister of Health's office. Kabul was really not my thing. It must have been my fourth or fifth time there, but it made me more and more nervous to be there.

On the previous mission, we had gotten to the airport and the power had gone out. The lines of passengers jockeying to get closer to the check in desk and people trying to scam others into letting them take their baggage to be scanned for security or to cut the queue to check in became a sinister shadow play. These things never seemed to bother my team leader. But he was the kind of person who got turned on to international development work as a young doctor working in Mogadishu when it was going to pot. That time, the lights finally came on, so the metal detectors were working again and they were ready to let people through immigration. Immigration officers with grim expressions and handguns in holsters asked for our papers. They scrutinized my thick American passport with some skepticism.

"You don't have stamp from the Ministry–Internal Affairs."

"I'm sorry, Sir?" I smiled at the officer. When confronted by officials, especially related to immigration, I start with a dumb pleasant girl smile. Excessive politeness and deference.

"The registration stamp? All foreigners must require to get stamp from the Ministry within three days of arrival." He held up three fingers in emphasis. "Where is your stamp?"

"Oh, is this a new requirement?" My heart sank. "I have never been asked for this stamp before." That didn't sound like a very good excuse not to have a stamp. "I'm with the World Bank. They didn't tell me to go the Ministry." I began to panic. My face got very serious.

"This has always been the requirement. Why you are in violation every time?"

I looked at my team leader for help. He was traveling on a UN passport, a Laissez-Passer. So he didn't have the same problem. He didn't say anything. He looked slightly amused. "This is my team leader. He will tell you that I'm here on an official mission for the World Bank." I shot him another look. Why isn't he pulling rank on this guy. But he just grinned at me. A five foot six, Italian imp. I began emergency planning. How was I going to get back to the World Bank guest house, how was I going to be in touch with Hamidullah to organize this exit stamp? How was I going to book the next flight out? No wait, I wasn't thinking clearly. I should figure out a way to get out of this situation now, and not miss my flight. Was there a way to pay a fee for this oversight and be done with this? That was smarter thinking. And when all those things had gone through my mind, the immigration officer waved me through.

"Next time, you must get the stamp."

"Yes, sir." I agreed wholeheartedly. I almost saluted him. Next time I would make sure I went straight from the airport to Internal affairs to get my paperwork done. But I was also thinking, next time, there wouldn't be a next time.

Once we were safely through the immigration gates, I turned to my team leader and hissed. "Why didn't you say anything?"

"It was so funny, my dear. You looked so scared. Like you were really going to be left behind." He started giggling, patting me on the back. He bought me a chai while I sulked a little. It really would have been a bad thing to have missed that flight.

And I returned again. I did the missions, because it was something I had invested a lot of technical thinking into, I liked the team leader, and there was an Australian based in Kabul who occasionally afforded sex on the side. Some reasons were better than others. This mission had been particularly stressful. There had been more restrictions than usual about which restaurants people were allowed to go to due to security threats. The weather brought smeary gray slush. It was December, there was no heat at the Ministry. The government staff worked with their coats on, making silent excuses to be next to the small space heater in the cavernous uninsulated rooms. People attended our meetings if only to enjoy the body heat of others in the room, the breath of the last speaker hung in the air like the notes of a spectral secretary keeping the minutes.

After working together for several months, I had only during this mission discovered that my counterpart in the ministry, someone I was counting on to run some quantitative studies for the project, did not know how to do long division or interpret fractions. I guess when you're living through a war that lasts for thirty years, making people into doctors is a priority and it's not critical if those people missed most of fourth grade and all the requisite math. Emanuele was working on two different financial agreements during this mission, so I had been working mostly by myself. Upon reaching the guesthouse the night before, Emanuele had excused himself to vomit before sitting down to dinner.

It took forty-five minutes for Hamidullah to get back to us with an update. The UN flight to Dubai the next morning had a seat. But only one. The Air India flight back through Delhi was scheduled to resume the next afternoon. It was flying an extra plane to make up for the stranded passengers. But there was no reason given for why it had been canceled today and it wasn't completely clear whether the problem had been or would be resolved for tomorrow's flight. Upon hearing the options, my team leader gave me a look to see what I wanted to do. He was being a gentleman. He was being a team leader, prepared to be the last one left on the ship, if need be. It was second nature to him to let me take the first flight out.

"No, you go ahead. Book the UN flight. The girls are waiting for you," I said. "The other flight is only another couple of hours. It will be fine." I wasn't really convinced. I was preparing myself to be spending Christmas in Kabul. It would be sadder than going to Boston Chicken and then boarding a Greyhound bus on Thanksgiving night, but I had done that before. A long time ago when I was a student, a rank even lower than single, working person.

"Yes, but if there's a problem..." He made a gesture of chaos with his eyebrows and shoulders. He was acknowledging the risk.

"Just go. Don't worry about it." And I could see the relief on his face, when he saw that my offer was firm. He had a family. He needed to get on that plane. People were waiting for him. He had a unit to reunite with. And that could not be said of me. In any case, I got out of Kabul on that next flight. It was a relief, but as the plane lost contact with the runway, the dark feeling of being alone descended over me. Flying home but not to anyone in particular, I was a single node with an uncertain connecting point. A small point of light in the sky, that disappeared with an inadvertent shift in view.

KINDNESS AND STRANGERS

"AND WHO WILL BE PICKING YOU UP THAT DAY?" My IVF coordinator looked at me, ready to record my response on my IVF Plan of Action. I guessed she didn't bother to ask the question of her client most of the time and just started writing down the name of the husband, the wife, the partner, the person who had been coming to all the visits with the client. I didn't have that person. I didn't have an answer for her. "Your mother? Your sister?" she suggested. Both of mine were thousands of miles away. My hesitation made us both uncomfortable.

"Don't you have any friends?" The question was meant to be kind. Helpful. The way you ask a dementia patient where they lived. It wasn't a hard question. But the only thing that came to my mind was, "Loser. Now she thinks I'm a loser."

I had been sticking needles in my stomach for the past two weeks, as per the schedule. They were thin needles that went in subcutaneously. Angled sideways, not with the urgent stabbing of an EpiPen into your thigh, but still it felt like self-harm of some kind. The day of the Harvest was coming closer. And just a half hour ago, Dr. Will had proclaimed my ovaries teeming with eggs. We counted them together on the fuzzy gray screen. Nineteen. I felt like I had aced a test. I wanted to wear a sticker on my chest, like the one they give you after you donate blood. My sticker would proclaim that I was a fully validated fertile person, stimulating hormones notwithstanding. Score one for those of advanced maternal age.

But in the meeting with my IVF coordinator directly after—I was not even fully dressed—my glow quickly faded. The day of the Harvest I would be undergoing general anesthesia. The clinic could not let me go home alone, they needed to release me to a designated person, who had to watch me for the rest of the day. Who was it going to be? Who would take care of me? Accept responsibility for me? Who could I ask?

"I'll have to get back to you," I said. I needed to get out of there. I stuffed my bare feet in my half-tied shoes and grabbed the socks off the floor, shoved them in my purse, the way I wanted to hide the other unsightly things that had been exposed in that room. In the space labeled, "Released to:" my IVF coordinator began writing "Unknown." She wore the same look of pity as the medical examiner on Law & Order when they can't find a relation to claim the dead girl dredged up from the river. I needed to get out of the glare of that light that exposed my sad personal life. A single woman—an older single woman, trying to have a baby. Probably just trying to conceive a life companion for her old age. A modern-day Miss Havisham.

The bright light outside made me squint. I stopped to get my bearings. I headed toward the Piers, the sound of gulls fighting for scraps from tourists' lunches. I scanned the Embarcadero for a cab. What was I going to do? At that moment, I just wanted to be picked up and taken away. To go somewhere protected and think this through. I told myself I was a resourceful person. But the feeling that comes with realizing you're not fully prepared for something was a stone in my stomach.

The conversation with my IVF coordinator really threw me. I was not expecting to doubt myself before getting pregnant. Getting pregnant was supposed to be the easy part. A logistics nightmare, yes, but emotionally straightforward, just as I had handled everything else in my life, up to that point.

I had planned it all out. The financial bit. The legal bit. Thinking through all the scenarios. What I would do. What my contingency plan was. I knew if I had to involve other people, I would orchestrate it carefully, minimizing who needed to know, what, and when. Other people were obstacles to maneuver around. I had made up my mind to make this baby and I didn't have time to deal with other people's uncertainty, questioning, disbelief. It was a risk to talk about it too much with other people. What if their uncertainty, questioning, and disbelief infected me? Then what? There wasn't a contingency for dealing with doubt.

And now there was this problem. I needed to rely on someone. It was just for an afternoon, but it became a huge existential question for me. I always saw myself as someone who had no genius for any particular thing, but who was thoroughly competent. Self-sufficient.

This was devastatingly pointed out to me once in college by a guy I had sort of pined after. There were a few weeks, maybe two, when Ernie and I started getting friendly. We would go for large orange juices at Au Bon Pain in the Square, late at night, and talk. He was kind of a silent jock type, an Econ major, a "my body is a temple" kind of guy. But over orange juice, he opened up, told me about being raised by a single mom, a pet fish he'd had since grade school, still alive that he visited when he went home to his mother's place in Jersey. I thought we were becoming close. I was waiting for someone to make a move. Maybe I would surprise myself. And then one night, while we were sitting and drinking juice, he said he had to tell me something. I was totally unprepared.

"I guess," Ernie took a thoughtful sip of juice, "you should know that Tisha and me, we've started going out." Tisha?!? I bit down on the straw to keep my mouth from hanging open. Tisha was another girl in our dorm, a mousy pre-med. A chubby Korean girl. Pleasant enough, but bland as a frozen bagel. What the hell! I sat there stunned by this development. Even he knew that I needed an explanation. I was half listening, I kept thinking about all the other girls in our dorm, more interesting, better looking, more attractive than me, let alone Tisha. He acknowledged that this decision to start dating Tisha would mean no more late-night juice with me. And then he got to the heart of it.

"The problem with you," he said, "is that you don't need anybody. You're totally self-sufficient. With Tisha, it's different." He paused, looked at me. I didn't say anything. "Tisha relies on me. She started going to the gym with me. She's all motivated now. She's becoming a better person. I like that. I feel important." He finished with a smile, took a sip of juice, satisfied. And all I could think was, *WTF?*

But now sixteen years later I gotta say, Ernie, you kind of nailed it. That was exactly how I led my life.

I had my own house. I juggled six or seven contracts with different agencies at a time. I could go on a two-month trip to eight countries with only a 22-inch rolling bag and a carry-on. I was totally competent at managing my life, or at least the way it used to be. And that was how I planned on having this baby. On my own. That was the way the plan was supposed to go.

That's what I thought. Except that no matter how hard I tried, it was turning out that I really did need other people. Strangers and otherwise. Feeling my self-sufficient, independent self, sloughing away as I was trying to make this baby, that was what was so painful in this process.

I had gone into this baby project knowing I would have to stop traveling, that I would probably have to find a new field of work, that I would have to give up my old life and take a regular job with benefits, give up my house and move to

Honolulu. I was ready to give all those things up. It was the responsible thing to do. It is what everyone would expect. But giving up my sense of self too? I had not been ready for that.

It started with the donor. I needed him. That really didn't seem like it could be helped. But when I made that decision to involve him, I was determined not to make it a slippery slope. He was just going to give me the sperm. No strings attached. I chose a fertility clinic where he lived so he could make donations without duress. I didn't even crash at his apartment. I stayed at a hotel or short-term rental. I didn't ask him to come with me to any appointments. I would pay for the testing, the cryo-storage, everything but the gas money to drive to the clinic and produce the specimens. When he had difficulty getting to the clinic when the lab was open, I got instructions about how to transport his goods tucked into my shirt to maintain vial to skin contact to keep his guys at a comfortable temperature. The donor was a very good friend, but I was doing this on my own.

Now I had to ask him whether he could pick me up after my procedure. Maybe that was okay. He was already involved, if not invested. So, I called him. He picked up the phone, but he said he was scheduled to work and was going to be in the East Bay that morning. He could try switching with someone but he didn't know whether he could get coverage at such short notice.

"No big deal," I lied. "Just let me know." I hung up the phone. I was going to have to ask somebody else to get involved.

It wasn't that I didn't know anyone in the Bay Area. I knew a lot of people in the Bay Area. Some of my closest friends were in the Bay Area. I have a ton of family in the Bay Area. But nobody in my extended family knew my plan yet, so asking a cousin to help me would require a general announcement to the whole clan. I wasn't quite ready for that. There was my friend Judith, who lived in the East Bay. But she traveled incessantly for work and had to leave the day after The Harvest. She probably had a ton of errands to do before leaving, and coming over the bridge at rush hour to pick me up from the clinic and deposit me somewhere else—it felt like too much of a favor. On principle, I decided that Bridge traffic knocked out everyone who lived in the East Bay.

Then there was my college roommate, Alison, who lived in the city. A woman I had lived with all four years of college. We lived in the same city for four years during grad school. I introduced her to her husband. I was a bridesmaid in her wedding. I had just seen her for dinner a few days before. She knew I was going through my first IVF round. She was a doctor in reproductive health and knew exactly what was involved. Why hadn't she been the first person I thought of? It seemed obvious that I should pick up the phone and ask her.

But I couldn't.

I told myself it was an imposition. She had a three-year-old and was at that moment eight months pregnant. She was probably scheduled to work that morning, or didn't have child care. How could I ask her to schlep down to the fertility clinic to pick me up?

But that wasn't it. I wasn't being thoughtful or excessively polite. The truth was, I would have to shed my pride to make that call. To admit that I couldn't do it by myself. And I panicked. If I couldn't do this, what made me think I could handle the rest? I didn't want to admit that to myself. There was another ugly feeling tied up with that one. It didn't feel so good to be trying to do this on my own. I didn't feel liberated and empowered. It was hard. It made me feel lonely. And pathetic. And I didn't like other people knowing that.

You grow up being taught about the golden rule. That you should do unto others as you would have others do unto you. Be nice. Be helpful. I liked being nice. I liked being helpful. I guess I liked being thought of as nice and helpful. I was pretty good at both. But it was surprising how hard it was for me to be on the other side. I hated to ask for help. I didn't realize how much I avoided it. I hated to be the person in need.

But I packed those feelings away, I tied them up tightly, put it in a box and buried it. *Stop being a wimp*, I told myself. This isn't the first thing and it certainly wouldn't be the last thing I was going to have to do that was hard. Get used to it. No, get happy about it, or just give up. Parenthood was going to be a really long road. This was the time to get tough.

And then it dawned on me that this was the United States of America. I was going to a fancy fertility clinic. Surely, I could pay someone to pick me up from the clinic and babysit me for an hour and then get their tip and let me take a nap for the rest of the day. It wasn't really relying on strangers, if you paid them. In fact, this made me feel more self-sufficient. Everything in this process could be afforded in one way or another. So, I made a call.

My IVF coordinator paused a bit, surprised that I asked. I heard it in her voice, *Did I really not know anyone that would care for me?* I let it pass. But she said yes, there was a Rent-A-Nurse service that could be arranged. It was a bit expensive, she warned. No surprise to me. The idea that everything came with a large additional cost was something I was already used to. Or sort of used to. Everyone knows being a parent is expensive. It stood to reason that being a single parent would feel more expensive. A single woman trying to get pregnant was the most expensive of all. I was affording the whole thing; how could I not afford independence too? I took down the names of several Rent-A-Nurse services.

I began to read the yelp reviews for the different referrals I got from the clinic. And then an email came through from my college roommate:

> Hi VA,
>
> It was great to see you Saturday. I shouldn't have eaten those enchiladas. GI reflux all night long! Blahck, this is the worst stage of pregnancy. I hope you're feeling good. I was just wondering how things were going. Do you have someone to pick you up from the clinic after your procedure? They have to knock you out, don't they? It's no problem for me to come. What time is your appointment? I don't have to be at the clinic until 2:30.
>
> Let me know.
>
> Love,
>
> A

A short chirpy note. But reading her email by myself in my little rented room, I started to cry. I was feeling really alone in a city where I had good friends, I even had my college roommate. But I felt like I had to do things alone and get used to it and like it, because I had chosen it and I planned it that way, and I couldn't admit that what I really wanted was someone to do it with me.

It turned out I had a friend, who didn't know how alone I felt and had just sent an email to say casually, did I need anything? Because that is what friends do. And I really did need it.

This feeling of being alone though not really being alone came again and again. I was slow to realize it, slow to say out loud. I needed help. I wanted help. I had help, and I should avail myself of it and not feel bad about taking it.

That disconnect of living bodily in one reality, but telling myself a different story about what was going on, reminds me of another incident during that trip to Pakistan. One night during that week at the Serena, I was talking to my sister on Skype in my hotel room. She didn't know I was in Islamabad. She thought I was calling from Bangkok. She probably imagined I had just come back from the hotel pool or a Thai massage. We were chatting and gossiping. What should we get for my mother's birthday? How our parents were addicted to Korean soap operas. I was lying through my teeth how the meeting in Bangkok was going, when I heard some commotion outside the window. It sounded like gun fire and yelling, but far away, muffled.

The windows of the hotel were thick, probably double-paned. Not just the sound-proofed windows common in five-star hotels to keep out street noise, but probably reinforced glass that could withstand minor explosions or small munitions. It was hard to tell what was making the noise, but I thought it could have been a terrorist attack waged on the fortress, in the go-cart lanes below. Or maybe it was a demonstration of some kind and there were protesters, maybe the government was exerting extreme crowd-control and things were getting out of hand.

This was all happening while I continued talking to my sister on Skype. We were just using the audio, not video. I had told my sister it was because my connection wasn't super great. I continued to complain about my parents. I didn't mention my concern to her because there weren't supposed to be terrorist attacks in Bangkok. I was carrying on this conversation with my sister about how you couldn't talk to our parents during primetime anymore, but my mind was racing in another direction. If the hotel was under siege and there were going to be more guns or other weapons involved, it might be better for me to be barricaded under the desk in the room. So I moved the computer to the floor and sat with my back against the wall under the ornate curved legs of the table. There I was, talking to my sister about nothing, waiting for people to burst into the room and take me as a hostage. It all seemed reasonable at the time, to both continue talking and prepare for an attack. *That's what competent people do,* I thought at the time. It turns out, maybe that's what single moms do too.

Give It Up

As it turned out, pregnancy was a probability of 1 for me. That December, I was only a month into it. I walked around gingerly with my arms slightly away from my body, ready to hunch down and block any abdominal blow. I was in protective mode afraid someone would pop my belly and I'd find my hopes and dreams deflated all at once.

So that December, after my first IVF round, I didn't send out Christmas cards as I normally do. I picked up the practice from my father, who unilaterally wrote the family Christmas letter when we were growing up. In the old days, it used to be written in the traditional format: opening paragraph of well wishes, then one paragraph for each member of the family and then closing with some generic sign off wishing people well in the New Year. But then at some point, maybe after we went to college, my dad started doing these photo montages. Cutting and pasting photos by hand, covering a whole 8.5 x 11 sheet. At first, they showed members of the family at special events during the year, or times that we actually got together as a family, now that my sister and I were out of the house. Then he started adding inane captions to the photos, often as if spoken by one of his cats, bordered by pictures of flowers he grew in his garden. I think at first using pictures was a shorthand way of providing an update, but then it became his art. There was a point in time when the letters were perfect, informative and funny, visually interesting, but then I think they just got a little bit cuckoo. Especially when my sister started having children and his letters could depict babies and cats in dialogue or providing snarky commentary about the world. I often wondered what the recipients of these cards thought when they received the Loo Family Christmas card. Some of these people had met my father in college or grad school. That was fifty years ago.

If you took the whole collection and lined them up chronologically, it might give you a time lapse view of someone going gradually insane. Or possibly the unfolding of the life of a man who has reached the point of totally enjoying his life.

I started writing my own letter when I moved to India in 2004 because I felt far away and needed to update people with my whereabouts and state of mind. By then I had collected a group of friends I liked to stay in touch with, but didn't see very often. There were friends from high school, then college, then grad school. There were people on the East Coast, West Coast, Hawai'i, and Atlanta. Some overseas. The first year, I wrote my letter sitting at a gate at the Indira Ghandi Airport. It was the middle of the night, like all the international flights I've ever taken from Delhi. I was flying home after six months in India. I had turned 30 that October, but I still felt like I was in college flying home for the holidays. Maybe it was that unspoken feeling of relief to be going home and the moment of mildly entertaining the idea of "maybe I won't come back." That time, embarking on a long-haul flight always makes me contemplative, it was a good mood to be in to write an interesting holiday note.

I admit, my holiday letter/monologue is written to a general audience. I type it up and print the same letter for everyone on my list and then I write something specific to the person at the bottom in pen, later. It's a different kind of exercise to write a letter to a group of people, rather than an individual. I have a diverse group of friends, collected from very different life stages and contexts, but the letter I write has to be recognizably from me as perceived by everyone who receives it. That can be a tough letter to write if you feel you've evolved at all over a 15-20-year period.

So that year, being barely pregnant, I didn't write anything. I wasn't ready to tell people. Really, you're not supposed to tell people until after your first trimester. In case. But even besides all that general miscarriage concern, I wasn't ready to tell people that I was pregnant. I wasn't ready to have the exchange with people, especially people whose last update was the last Christmas letter I had sent.

"Hey, I have exciting news, I'm pregnant!!!"

"Oh, wow, that's amazing." The look of "What?!?!?" on their faces, "I didn't even know you got married."

"I'm...I didn't!"

"Oh, wow, umm...."

A look of "What?!?!?" all over their faces.

"That's...amaz— great!"

"Yeah, thanks."

"Okay, wow."

A look to the side, with eyes that say "Did you just hear the same thing I heard?!?!"

I wasn't sure where the conversation was going to go after that. How much to explain. How much backstory to give. How much about how I was feeling about everything. How much of the timeline to give people.... Putting all that in a holiday letter didn't seem quite right. This was something I wanted to tell people in different ways, not through a mass mailing. And not yet. Writing a holiday letter giving an update about everything else going on, but omitting the fact that there was an occupant in my uterus seemed not in the spirit of a Christmas letter. So, I didn't send one that year.

I rode pregnancy into the new year the way Santa Claus rides into Waikiki Beach in a double hulled catamaran paddled by a team of hunky elves. I didn't have feelings of nausea or lose my appetite. For some reason, I craved whole grains. I lived in comfy clothes (which were the same as the clothes I wore before I got pregnant) and ate almost whatever I felt like. The early months of pregnancy were almost the same as the months prior to.

At the end of my first trimester, I had my first work travel since getting impregnated. The trip was to Laos where I joined a team of two other expat consultants doing site visits to remote districts. At that point, I hadn't shared with any colleagues that I was pregnant, it didn't seem relevant to the work. Until we discussed the logistics of getting to these villages tucked into the mountains near the border of China. The transport options were to take a minivan or a prop plane to reach our mountain destination. The flight was deemed just over the line of unsafe due to poor landing conditions and the relative instability of the airline operating the flights. But the van ride would take six hours along a narrow road weaving through the mountains.

In the end, the project director arranged for a van so we could make the road trip. We took switch back after switchback, it felt unending. We planned to stop halfway in a valley town for something to eat. No one was really hungry but we were relieved to take a break. I was impressed that I had made it that far without feeling sick, but I really needed to find a bathroom. One guy on the team said, "I think we should just push through. Let's just get this travel done with."

But then the project director, a usually gentle and accommodating lady, said "No," very firmly. "The driver needs to rest." Her serious tone was sobering and a reality check. This wasn't just a casual drive out to the village. Quickly, everyone agreed that was a good idea, the driver should take as much time as he wanted.

As we staggered out of the van, we assessed the road stop's amenities. The parking area was the largest flat cleared area we had seen in several hours. It looked like it could accommodate eight or nine large sized tour buses, though it seemed unlikely that a bus that size could make it around the turns in the road without toppling over the edge. In any case, this was clearly the main rest stop for this mountain road. We spied one open stall of a restaurant, a market selling drinks, snacks, and detergent, and across the way, a large raised concrete platform bathed in sunlight featuring an open-air green market. Two ladies, who may have been in competition with each other, had laid out their display featuring a few clumps of mountain spinach and bunches of dried chili peppers. To the side a group of skinny dogs napped, exposing their bellies upward as if they were solar panels collecting the day's energy.

I ordered thick wheat noodles—Chinese-style, and someone else ordered some type of organs in an angry red sauce—a local specialty. I claimed to be vegetarian. While waiting for the food, I browsed a reasonably recent issue of the Vientiane Times, left on one of the tables. It featured an article about the road we were on. It claimed that this part of Highway 3 was the twistiest road in Laos that numbered several hundred switchbacks and was notorious for having the most road accidents per kilometer in the region. The article ended by advocating road safety policy change. I passed the article around to my travel companions and we all smiled ruefully. Next time, we are taking the plane, my team mate said with conviction.

And then we piled back in the van. In many years of rough road travel, I had never gotten car sick. Not in the thousand hills of Rwanda, not in the misty roads of Ooty in India. There was one time in Uganda on the road from Kampala to Entebbe, but it was mostly due to a bad samosa. I was determined to make it the rest of the journey without incident, and not having to play the pregnancy card. As everyone else finished their lunch, I ventured over to the shop front next door and bought a load of salty snacks and ginger candies, bottles of water. The mountain air was thin enough that the bags of chips had inflated and seemed ready to pop. We were still driving up the mountain, which meant the cliff-side of the road. So, I played the lady card and got offered a window seat in back of the driver. And because it was very clear that our lives were in his hands, I made sure to ply the driver with snacks to make sure he stayed awake and alert for the rest of the drive.

Despite the remoteness of the mountain, it was a busy road, there being only one way up and one way down. Though the cool mountain air coming in from the window helped, it was mixed with the sickening exhaust from the cars and trucks ahead. As a compromise, I closed the window and lay my cheek against the cool glass. When we arrived, the village was already dark and the night air made me shiver. I layered several shirts and sweaters on top, and pulled on two pairs of pants. I had packed for humid jungle weather not the top of mountains. I could have used a nip of liquor to warm up before bed like the rest of the team, but abstained. Nothing is more lame than being a teetotaling vegetarian on a trip like that. That night I dreamed I was somersaulting back down the mountain, tucked up like an armadillo to protect my belly, except instead of flesh and skin my torso was a swelling bag of chips.

Somehow the trip was completed, both up and down the mountain without any vomiting and without me having to reveal my pregnancy to get special consideration. I felt proud of my professionalism and my travel hardiness. Several years later, I saw one of the other expat team members from the van. As we caught up, he told me his partner had been pregnant during that trip to Laos too. I was surprised, because this guy was much older and had already had grown children when I met him. So this was his second round of parenting. The conversation was so friendly, we empathized with each other about being consultants in the same line of work and trying to balance work travel with parenting young children. It was great to think that he was feeling the same push and pull of struggle and enjoyment.

I felt normal and encouraged. Men and women all go through the same feelings. I felt this moment of comforting camaraderie. Or gender equality. But then when I thought about it some more, I thought *No. It is not really the same.* We may have both been on that trip coming to grips with how much more unpredictable life was going to be in another six months. We might both have been on the brink of losing it in the van that week, but I was the one with a fetus vibrating in my abdomen. It. Was. Completely. Different.

In theory, being pregnant shouldn't have been a big deal to share with the people hiring me. But I worried. Being a consultant, I often felt out of sight, out of mind. A key part of my ability to get a steady stream of work is popping up at regional meetings, or joining teams sponsored by multiple UN organizations. Meeting and re-meeting lots of different people meant people might think of me when they were looking for a consultant. Letting a large group of people know I was pregnant might make people think I wasn't going to be available for future work. For a while.

Flexibility is another important characteristic. The kind of consultant contracts I take get negotiated over short periods of time. If some agency has money they need to spend down, they want a consultant who can commit to work and get it done and bill them before the money gets re-appropriated. Pregnant people are not known to be very flexible. Nor are people with newborns. So even though I wasn't flexible and was planning to take some time off, I didn't want other people to know that. Better to say I was not available, letting people assume that I had other work commitments. Better to seem highly in demand, than totally incapacitated.

I didn't know exactly what I was going to do for income after having this baby. I suspected that maintaining this work life I had was a no-go. Probably, I should start thinking about a more conventional job, no travel, with regular hours and benefits. But I wasn't so sure how viable that was either. I made a much better living as a consultant than I might with the salaries I might get with 9-to-5 work. I hadn't done a formal job interview since working at CDC. I didn't really know what kind of work was available to a person like me in Hawai'i. I wasn't sure I was ready to change fields completely. I wondered how much easier it would really be to make a living with a full-time job-job and be a single mom of a little kid? I wasn't sure which was the right way to go. Choosing to continue to be an independent consultant felt like being a pregnant lady deciding to drive a minivan up a mountain road. It was tempting to opt to take a plane. It wasn't obvious what would be the safer bet.

The last work trip I did was in April. By then, I had come to the conclusion that I should find another line of work after the baby was born. Traveling with a small kid wasn't tenable and I decided that without being able to travel I wasn't as valuable to the people hiring me. After this trip I would start my informational interviewing, thinking about new fields of work. Even if it required starting over, I would do what I had to do. So I scheduled back-to-back assignments hitting several countries. On this last trip, I would finish up a number of projects and earn as much as I could in the time I had before birthing. And then I would say goodbye to all of it. This was my farewell tour.

I told colleagues that I was going to have a baby and would be taking time off from travel. By then, my pregnancy was fairly obvious, so talking about it was not a big admission. I got warm wishes, but also puzzled faces from people who had on previous trips thoroughly explored the idea that I was not married and not living with my parents. Before I had left for this last trip, my sister had suggested I wear a ring on my left hand. "You're going to a socially conservative country; do you think people will be offended if you're pregnant and not married?" I'm not sure what she thought someone would do if they were offended for that reason. Maybe she thought immigration control wouldn't honor my visa. In my mind, the worst thing that would happen is that they would decide they did not want to engage me as a consultant any more.

On the second to last stop I saw Oscar, who had by now moved to Jakarta and had brought me in to work on projects there just as he did in Burma. He lived in a big highrise perched above a fancy shopping mall. It was directly across the street from the hotel I stayed at when I came for work. When I was in town, I could take the pedestrian bridge across the massive six lane road between us to hang out at his place. That last night I was in Jakarta, Oscar invited me over to have dinner at their apartment. His partner took extra care to serve hard cheeses instead of soft and cooked vegetables. The other guests were asked to smoke on the balcony to avoid poisoning my unborn child with their second-hand smoke. It was a fun evening and I got up to go back to the hotel. Then Oscar said he would walk me over the pedestrian bridge. On the way down the elevator, I asked him why, since he had never done it before. And he said, "Actually some people have gotten mugged on the bridge late at night." I gave him the look as in "how come you never told me that before?!?" And he smiled sheepishly, in his way, and said, "It doesn't happen *thaaaat* frequently. But still, since you're going to be a mother..." And then he cackled.

We got to my end of the bridge, where Oscar thought I would be reasonably safe. And before heading down the long flight of stairs that stopped in front of the hotel, he gave me a hug. "I don't know when I'll see you next."

In my head, I thought, *Probably never.* I was going to miss Oscar and the buffet breakfasts at four-star hotels, the thinking time afforded by long flights, taking team trips on mountain roads. Maybe most of all being regarded as an expert in my field.

Suddenly, having a baby seemed like such a non-sequitur in my life. I stood at the top of the pedestrian bridge looking down over a large, round belly, I could barely see the step under my feet. I felt like a ball held high in the air. A ball about to be let go.

HARD TO SAY

I GOT PAST MY FIRST TRIMESTER, when it should be safe to
share my news with others, but I wasn't sure. What exactly
was I going to tell my extended family? Some people knew,
some people were still in the dark. Keeping everything out
in the open seemed like the best policy, because not saying
anything might make people think that the situation wasn't
kosher. Plus having an unequal distribution of information
within my family just encouraged gossip. That's a law of
physics and family: moving bodies collide in an unrelenting
pursuit of chaos, achieving stability in the lowest state
of energy; in other words, everybody commenting on
everybody else's business until it's old news and everybody
settles down.

Email seemed the most egalitarian method of telling
people the news. Everybody could see who else got the news.
Everybody got the same text, if not the same take-home
message. Like balls in a rack on a pool table, I gathered my
cousins, aunts, and uncles on a distribution list. I composed
my subject line: "Sharing some news." I tried to apply email
tips I had learned from work: keep it short, put the main
message in the first sentence, review the recipients two or
three times. I pressed "Send," let loose the break shot and
waited to see where all the balls went.

I took in the responses keeping a little distance, unsure
how fast and hard the ricochet would be. I got some nice,

encouraging messages. Much of it was commensurate with other congratulatory emails circulated to married cousins announcing upcoming children. A few run-of-the-mill good wishes were "Reply All," as much a message to the whole family on where people stood, as well as to me. There were a few notes with extra special messages of support and seconding the idea that this was a good time to do something about my situation. And then there were marked silences. One family didn't send any acknowledgement of the email. They had school-aged kids. Maybe it was going to be an awkward thing to explain. Their silence might have been disapproval, or discomfort, or just hectic lives.

I got one "congratulatory" phone call from a cousin. He chortled his total surprise, frankly. He jokingly asked whether this was "a love child or something." Ooooh, that cavalier comment hit me like a pool ball in the side of my head. I wanted to say, "Hey, go back and read my email, Buddy. I explained it all in the email!" Then I went back to read my own email for vindication, but found, oh yeah, I didn't mention the donor or the mechanics of what happened. I wasn't very specific about what I thought was going to happen in the future raising my kid. It really required people to be able to read between the lines. Actually, it was a pretty unforthcoming email.

What I had meant to convey was the part about this being a very deliberate and planned pregnancy. This being in the works for some time. This baby, as a product of IVF, had cost me quite a bit of money. It was not a shot in the dark or a one-night stand. It was not an act of serendipity.

Why was it so important to me that people understood the effort and the resources I had invested so far? I wanted people to know I had made a real calculation about whether and how to have a baby. That it wasn't without some sacrifice. Maybe my baby wasn't going to have a dad, but I was trying really hard to do the thing right. That probably was the message I wanted people to get.

It was an announcement about having a baby, but I was trying to tell people that the way I was doing it was "doing it right." My sensitivity to the stigma of "illegitimacy" was stronger than I admitted. What my family thought of me, and how I fit in with them mattered more than I wanted. Which is worse: being the spinster in the family or the unwed mother? Hard to say. Having opened up myself to my family's judgment. I felt stung when some of them actually chose to judge.

So much for my open-door policy. It is hard to have it both ways: giving the appearance of transparency and maintaining privacy. At the same time, you want to say "I have nothing to hide," but you're also not willing to share that you have holes in your underwear, your innermost thoughts.

After I sent the email, my sister and parents got a few calls from family members. *What exactly was going on? Who was the father? How did this happen?* When they told me about the calls, I said indignantly, "The family should feel free to ask me directly. There's no problem with asking."

My mouth was saying, "*I am open to discussing everything.*" But my gut put two hands up front and wildly gestured "*No Comment.*" People could probably sense that. My parents said in the future they would refer family questioners back to me. "Fine," I told them, "But feel free to answer their questions too."

Ughhh. I felt so uncomfortable talking about it with my family. Contemplating face-to-face conversations made my heart pound. My family is great when being critical, breaking things down, being argumentative. They get feisty and tell you exactly what they think. Had I brought it up with them at the beginning of this process when I was making some difficult decisions, I would have had a thousand loud opinions of what they thought. And now that I was far along this path, I still didn't think I could handle it. I was really hoping for someone to take up the role of being my spokesman. I dreaded questions about what I was thinking. "Why did you decide to do this?" "How are you going to manage this?" How much should I reveal? How much should I talk about my fears and doubts and crazy feelings?

Now I saw the value of the boilerplate language in my legal agreements with the donor. I should have quoted it in my email, "*I am excited and enthusiastic to share with you that soon I will be able to realize 'my greatest hopes and dreams of having a child.' Thank you for your unconditional love and support.*" That would have pre-empted conversation. Present a controversial fact and my family would dispute it. Confront my family with sentiment, start with the touchy feels, and they will smile politely and start to back out of the room. If I had said it that way, it wouldn't matter who the father was, or how it happened. Everybody would know that a new person in the family is coming and he or she expects all the privileges of membership.

"Hurry up, or we're going to be struck down by lightning," my sister whispered. She nudged my stomach and giggled. We were posing for selfies under a pretty stained-glass window in a Catholic church in Waikiki. We were at my cousin's wedding Mass and my seven-month baby belly was a prominent accessory.

"See if you can fit a quarter in your belly button," my sister had dared me earlier. "Do it. Do it! So you won't get that divot in the front of your dress." She laughed when I tried it. Now, we were in God's house. Taking pictures there in my unmarried and pregnant condition with loose change in my navel felt like trolling. Being a lifelong atheist didn't help either.

This was the second Catholic wedding in eight days that I had attended. At the first one, the DJ called all the single ladies to come up for the bouquet toss. I was tempted. My best friend from high school egged me on."Do it, do it." Give people another reason to talk about this wedding. People might say, "Remember how that massively pregnant lady clocked the eight-year-old so she could catch the bouquet so she could be next to get married. She must have really wanted it." I weighed the pros and cons.

I was willing to sacrifice some of my own dignity if I could go viral on YouTube and shame future brides from incorporating a bouquet toss into their weddings. Maybe for an eight-year-old the bouquet toss is the best part of the day, but to a single woman in her thirties, it's like the bride rubbing salt into the wounds of her unmarried friends. Surely the bride herself has had the humiliating experience of being called up by name by a jerk with a microphone to vie on a makeshift dance floor-gladiator pit, to claim a wilting bunch of used flowers. Why then would she incorporate this crazy ritual into her own nuptials, except that she is a cruel human being? It is really inhuman, I think. At the very least, unbecoming of the bride. Someone, a celebrity wedding planner, a Supreme Court Justice, a former Ambassador to the UN general assembly, maybe PETA, should stand up for single women attending weddings and recognize that this practice must be stopped.

As for *unbecoming*, I was seven months pregnant. I could not stop sweating; I had bags under my eyes from not sleeping and I struggled daily to find something to wear. I might be blacklisted from future weddings for life, I thought, but what the hell—if I could stand up fast enough, I would get my ass to the toss.

Yes. Okay. That was my fantasy self, talking out loud. I kept my seat. It was my friend's special day; it would have been unseemly to make a spectacle of myself in that way. More unseemly too because the dress I wore was not designed to be maternity wear. It fit because it was highly elasticized, but it did not adequately encase my boobs. My big belly hiked my dress up in the front to a precarious level. The exertion of reaching for a bouquet would likely result in the release of a larger than normal boob and potentially some gas. That might detract from the larger political point I was trying to make.

So that day, Prudence won over Infamy, though I can't guarantee that would be the case in the future. Besides, I reminded myself, I had another wedding to attend the next week, where there would be another chance to do it all differently.

At my cousin's wedding later that week, I sat at a table of the "Unmarrieds," an assorted group of unmatched socks: friends from high school, underage cousins, and me. As the bride's mother toured tables, greeting guests, she turned to me and nodded at my 13-year-old cousin, "I guess we'll have to wait for Kiki's turn until we celebrate the next family wedding."

"Hey," I interrupted, "what about me?!"

"Oh. Sorry," my aunt tittered, "Yes, I guess that's true..." She was Cinderella's step mother acknowledging to Prince Charming's emissary that yes, technically there was another woman of marriageable age in the house who could try on a shoe. Unwed mothers were not really a thing in my family. It took getting used to. Getting married after bearing your bastard child was not an idea my family had gotten its head around yet.

Did I mention it was also the week of my 20th high school reunion?

At the reunion I felt like a teenager coming back to school after summer vacation knocked up. I was nervous, not sure what I should say, not sure what people might say back. When you lead with your abdomen, it's going to come up in the conversation, no matter how long it has been since you've seen a high school friend. It seemed odd to talk about the pregnancy without getting into the interesting part of the backstory, but I didn't find an easy way to get into it.

"Hey, how are you? You look great. When are you due?"

"Thanks! I feel enormous. Seven more weeks to go."

"Wow, exciting! Is this your first?"

"Yes." I wanted to say something else. *I'm doing it on my own.* Did that come across as defensive? *It's a donor baby.* That seemed kind of abrupt. *The father is a good friend from college.* That didn't convey the main point. My eyes said, *Ask me about the father. You won't regret it. It will be the most interesting thing you hear today, or at least in your top five.* I waited for my conversations to go there. And they just didn't. I felt like I could burst.

I had gone to my 10-year reunion too. At that one, I had just finished my Ph.D. I was about to embark on a great post doc at the CDC. And I had thought then I had big things to talk about with people interested in a casual catch up.

People who go to reunions are self-selecting. They go because they want to be there and they are happily curious to hear what other people are doing, especially the people who go to a 10-year reunion. When you're 28, you still feel young but maybe you're also beginning to feel powerful in your workplace. That's what I remember.

The 20th reunion felt different. Maybe it was because of my age. By your late thirties, you're a bit further along in your career, maybe you have plateaued or feel a little stale. Maybe you are a bit more stressed, trying to balance your personal life too—married or remarried, on your second, maybe third kid. At that point, you may just be happy to have a night out, and besides seeing who has gained more weight than you, you don't really need to compare notes.

At some point that night, I sat at a table happily eating my dinner, and a classmate came up to congratulate me on the pregnancy. "I didn't know that you had gotten married," she exclaimed.

I looked up at her and mimicked her open mouth face of happy amazement, and answered back with the same level of giddy enthusiasm, "Oh, I didn't!" And smiled wide. Her face froze, her smile looked uncomfortable in its exuberance and deflated into a lowercase "o." It wasn't clear what an appropriate response might be. But her longtime boyfriend reached over from across the table and let out a hoot.

"Alright!" he said, "Hi-five!" and my palm met his with a satisfying slap. That could have been a high five for many things. For him, probably different than for me.

But that week included event after event involving meeting up with high school friends, the same set of high school friends, over and over again, actually. So I found myself telling bits of my story to various subsets. At one potluck dinner, I balanced a plate of fried chicken cutlets on my knees while explaining who my baby donor was, and I could see the head of another acquaintance sitting nearby, but not in our conversation, turn slightly toward us, to get the scoop. By the end of the week, my story, however shaped by semi-complete information and interested speculation, had gotten around. With each telling, I didn't know where to start and end, how much detail to give, who just wanted the big questions answered and who was interested in the minutiae. Some people were interested in the psychological process of choosing to be a single mom, the donor identity, the technical process of getting pregnant, the plan for where to live and how to make a living afterward, and then some just wanted the usual details you get on any pregnant woman—due date, sex, possible names. By the end of the week, I was tired of my own story. All of it.

Oh, and yeah, that was also the week I moved in with my parents.

The move was something I had planned for some time. And the week of the weddings and reunion were at the end of the period my OB thought I should be doing airplane travel. You never know with these high-risk births to people of advanced maternal age. The baby might come early.

One of my all-time favorite movies is *Auntie Mame* starring Rosalind Russell. It's a movie about a glamorous, swinging aunt who unexpectedly inherits a child from her uptight brother. It is a fabulous old Technicolor movie. I used to watch it with my dad when I was a kid. It's shot like theater, each scene fading out around the face of Mame, until the only thing decipherable is her Cheshire Cat grin or the whites of her eyes. I used to catch it on cable once or twice a year, until I bought a copy on DVD and could watch it anytime I wanted. I first got it when I lived in Atlanta and it followed me to India and then to Hilo. I still have it. It's Old Hollywood. Mame finds the love of her life, even while raising a 10-year-old on her own and losing all her money in the stock market crash of 1929. Her husband is filthy rich and he falls to his death because he can't stop taking pictures of her in exotic locations from precarious perches. And then later as her second husband she takes her best friend of thirty years. I think I always identified with Mame a little bit. Or had identified with her up until now. Having moved into my parents' house, I felt more like Agnes Gooch, Mame's awkward, hunchbacked secretary who introduces herself as "Gooch." (To be clear, she's not really hunchbacked, she has terrible posture. I identified with that too, having been yelled at by my mother about my posture all my life. She should have told me that I would regret it most when I was pregnant. There's nothing worse for your spine than being pregnant and having a slouch.)

In this fabulous movie I used to watch with my father, Gooch is impregnated but can't remember by whom. She remembers a dream about being in a Gary Cooper movie where someone is getting married, and then she starts to cry because she remembers she herself remains unwed. Later, Agnes is seen going up and down a grand staircase in a heavily pregnant state by Mame's prospective in-laws. When they ask Agnes about "Mr. Gooch" and it turns out there is none, they are horrified that Mame would harbor a woman in sin. But all ends well for Agnes, kind of. She remembers who the father of her baby is, and that they already had gotten married—although the father only agrees to stick with Agnes and the baby so long as Mame gives him a regular allowance.

I thought of that movie a lot as, like Agnes, I navigated the stairs at my parents' house. I had to go up three flights of stairs to get to my room and down the same set of stairs to get to the kitchen. Then down a flight of stairs to get a good internet connection for work or doing teleconferences. I also came down from my room frequently for snacks.

Soon I began to assimilate myself into my parents' regular schedule. They went to discounted foreign movies on Tuesday afternoons, auction previews on Fridays, had a different Korean drama to watch every night, and twice monthly they played bridge with my senile great aunt.

Aunty Yung used to be sharp as a tack. She was a librarian and a tough Chinese lady. Her long arthritic fingers with the bulging knuckles could point out the flaw in the fish you were trying to pass off as fresh or the price that was asking "tooooo much!" Aunty Yung used to like to host a dinner whenever my sister's family was visiting from New Jersey. She scoured the local paper for the Chinese restaurant ads advertising banquet menus and when she found the deal she liked, she'd invite our family out. Throughout the meal she harangued the staff for stingy portions and inauthentic ingredients. She complained that nobody offered the right kind of red vinegar to eat with the crispy chicken. At the end of the meal, she would pay and we would all say, "Thank you Aunty Yung." And then she would count out a handful of dimes and nickels to leave as a tip. It was hard to say why she was so stingy, whether it was her memory that was so bad she couldn't remember what year we were in or it was just her expectations of good service. My brother-in-law would hang back while others helped Aunty Yung to the car, and he'd scoop up the change and leave a real tip for the waiters.

Aunty Yung was famous for letting someone know when they did a stupid thing, especially when you were her bridge partner. She had been known to rap adults on the knuckles for miscounting trumps. At the end of her life, she was amazing in a different way. She could still beat you at bridge, but she couldn't remember anything you said during the game. Everybody pretended she hadn't asked the same question every ten minutes, they just gave the same answer in the same tone of voice and played their cards, while she shook her head at the dumb move made by her partner. My parents put up with it, because she enjoyed herself so much.

Aunty Yung's son would drive her over. My mother would make a big lunch. And for a tiny Chinese lady, Aunty Yung packed it in. It was as if she hadn't eaten anything else all week. When Aunty Yung volunteered to make lunch, my father would pretend she cooked last time and say it was their turn to host.

Since I was then living with them, I was invited down to eat the bridge luncheon my mother served. Over crab cakes and corn chowder, the conversation took a bad turn. It unfolded like a movie.

"Hi, Aunty Yung,"

She noticed my Gooch gut as I sat down, and looked puzzled.

"You're Virginia, aren't you?" I nodded. She stared into the middle distance, "I don't think I remember meeting your husband." Pause. "I remember your sister's husband. George, isn't it?"

"Yes, Aunty Yung," starting with the affirmation, "Eleanor's husband's name is George." Pause. "But I'm not married."

"Oh, I see." She turned to my father and gave him a look as if to say, *do you think this fish is fresh?* "So, who is the father of the baby?"

My father gestured back to me.

"Aunty Yung," I tried to break it to her gently. But where to start? "I'm having this baby on my own. I have a donor." I stopped. Would she even know what that meant? I didn't want to shock her. I didn't know how much detail to provide. Aunty Yung looked at me a little longer, to see if I was going to say anything more. Maybe that was enough?

"I haven't had *long an* in a long time," she said. "Did you know that Popo grew up at a house with a very famous *long an* tree? That fruit was so sweet. But something happened to it, one year it just stopped producing fruit. It was a great mystery. Popo's mother thought the neighbor might have poisoned it because she was jealous. Do you know who is living at that house now?" And then there was some talk about the lease on that property that was more than 70 years old, and yes, the tree was still there when my parents had visited a few years ago. But no, there weren't any fruit on it at that time.

Talking about Popo was always a safe topic. Popo was her mother, my dad's grandmother. Popo had ten children and then her husband got run over by a car and died when the youngest was a few months old. This Chinese lady raised the kids by herself, managed a fishpond, and sued her in-laws for trying to take away her business. She was one of 14 kids herself. Those were the days when they really knew how to make babies.

Then Aunty Yung turned to me, "What is the name of your husband again, I can't quite remember."

"Aunty Yung, my baby doesn't have a father. I went to a fertility clinic."

She wrinkled her brow.

"I'm not married, Aunty Yung." I tried to get back to more familiar territory. But that seemed only marginally successful.

It was like that movie *Groundhog Day*. I tried again and again to figure out what would get me out of that hell hole of questions. "My baby is a bastard, Aunty Yung." "I don't know who the father of my baby is." "It was an immaculate conception." "I think the father is Gary Cooper."

As the Buddha would say, according to Pema Chödrön, "Embrace this—an opportunity to touch the uncomfortable place. Shed your ego. Approach the situation without having a story." Maybe that's what is going on in Aunty Yung's mind. She had reached Nirvana. She approached every inquiry with fresh curiosity and embraced the resulting confusion. She would not give up.

My father found it very amusing.

"My husband's name is George. This will be our third child." That seemed the most effective way to answer her question. Aunty Yung seemed satisfied. It got us to a whole new topic of conversation, the names and ages of my two older children. And for the afternoon, I gamely appropriated my sister's life.

CRAZY GODS' EYES

I HAVE AN AUNT WHO HAS THREE KIDS and is a neonatologist. She gave me my first paid job during summers in high school. I would do data entry for a project on long-term outcomes of extreme low birth weight babies. These babies were the kind that left the hospital with patient files heavier than they would ever be. Many of them wouldn't make it. Once, over lunch that summer, I commented "It must be the worst thing in the world for a parent to lose a child."

And my aunt said, "No, the worst thing for a parent is dying when your children are still young."

"Really?!? Why would that be? Because you couldn't see your kids grow up?"

"No, because you wouldn't know that they would be okay."

At that time, I could only see it from the child's perspective, a much-shortened life, the inability to realize human potential. Not the parent's fear of being unable to keep your kid safe and happy. A lot of the time I was pregnant, I thought about what would happen to my baby if I wasn't around during their growing up.

This was part of my planning and disaster preparation because I was going to be a single parent. If something catastrophic happened to me there would be my parents and also my sister and her family to take up guardianship. But my baby would never have that second person who had equal and primary responsibility for them as I did. My child wouldn't have that other person to live with in a nuclear family way. I imagined the nuclear family as the child in the middle, as the unmoving protons and the parents as spinning electrons weaving a cocoon of energy around the center. Atomic, powerful, a fundamental stable unit.

Admittedly, there's supposed to be both protons and neutrons in the middle, so let us suppose, in this imagining, the protons are the children and the neutrons are something like family pets. And that makes traditional families in high income countries a group of helium atoms, since they have two electrons orbiting around two protons, a labradoodle and a cat named Mr. Mittens. I'm not sure where else that metaphor goes. But my preoccupation was figuring out how I could create the same dynamism and energy as a single electron.

I didn't want my kid to go through life in a bubble. But who wants their kid to experience trauma, I mean actual trauma—death, disease, disfigurement, not trauma in the colloquial sense of embarrassment, inconvenience, or disappointment. When you're pregnant it is easy to think about all the things that could go wrong for your kid. In the first trimester I worried about miscarriage, in the second trimester I waited for the results of genetic deficiency tests. In the third trimester, I thought my baby might turn over and go breach or get their head squashed by my too small pelvis. (Inadequate pelvic size on an Asian mother giving birth to a baby with a Caucasian father is a real issue, due to racial differences in expected head size. That was an FYI from my Caucasian donor who regularly witnessed this problem as a practicing anesthesiologist providing epidurals.)

Once I had the baby, there would be so many other things to consider: sudden infant death syndrome (SIDS), being on the autism spectrum, childhood drowning, swallowing pennies, dyslexia, eating laundry detergent pods. And then, of course, I thought about *Pet Semetary*, the only Stephen King movie I ever watched. It starts with a toddler getting run over by a semi-truck right in front of his house. I thought about how my parents had a Prius, which makes almost no sound when backing up. I thought a lot about small children being killed by family members because of that.

That kind of thinking becomes overwhelming. I wasn't hysterical, but those thoughts were in the back of my mind, running in a loop. The truth is I didn't miss having coffee during pregnancy due to the constant mildly elevated level of adrenaline in my bloodstream. And then, that made me worry too, because of the association found between maternal stress during gestation and poor long-term health outcomes among children.

It is perhaps unsurprising that I became a public health professional because thinking about risk comes so naturally to me and quantifying preventable risk is an epidemiologists' bread and butter. Thinking about risk is human. It is what everyone does subconsciously all day in some form or another: using a seatbelt, washing your hands, eating the leftovers that have been in the fridge since last week. Epidemiology is the science that correlates the risk or protective factor with the chance that you will get a disease, experience an injury, or develop a condition.

My first foray into epidemiology was pure serendipity. When I left college early to join the clinical trial in Thailand, I understood what we were doing to be "research," figuring out the best way to deliver a medication. I only realized halfway in that what we were doing was epidemiology. The professor I worked for decided he owed it to me to "home-school" me in epidemiology. He gave me a basic epi text to read and two afternoons a week we'd sit in the open hallway of the Chiang Mai University medical school building where we had obtained some office space. The hot season was beginning. With the breeze, it was cooler out there though you could smell the lab below where the med students dissected blackened cadavers. We sat for about two hours at a time and he would answer my questions about the chapter I had just read. It was a completely different environment for learning than I had ever had: open aired, one-on-one, self-directed.

Those were the days when email use was nascent and international calls were expensive. I had a clunky laptop to work from, and I had to walk a mile to the office to plug in to connect through dial up internet, log on to my university account and try to communicate with a boyfriend I had started dating just before I left. Nobody I knew in Thailand was a native English speaker except the 10-year-old son of this professor. My professor was French, but he had worked in the US so long, his son was a dual citizen.

In the Thai humidity, my brain was like a frog entering a warm bath and being softly boiled to death. My thought process slowed because all my oral communication was so concentrated and painstaking—both me trying to speak and understand Thai and being understood in English. I remember that whole experience in dreamlike vignettes, the smell of the embalming fluids eluting my memory. The chatter of medical students walking through hallways under our office. The image of wheeled examination tables left in the grass to be aired out in the sun, cadaver stains fading on the surface. And then I have an out of body memory, an aerial view of myself walking along *Chon Prathan*, a four-lane road divided by a canal. I wear a large straw hat, a T-shirt that always feels damp, and a sarong. In this dream or memory, I have the perspective of the sun, heating the black road and the dry canals walls, making the metal edges of cars glint like knives.

In this memory of myself, I am at once the most Thai and not Thai. The T-shirt and skirt combo is very local, especially when wearing rubber thongs. But nobody in Thailand commutes by walking in the hot season. Everybody in Chiang Mai takes a *rot daeng*, a red truck, with an open-ended truck bed, lined with benches under a canvas canopy. You flag it on the side of the road and tell the driver where you want to get dropped off. It's cheap and efficient. Except when I tried it, my accent was so bad the driver would misunderstand me and I'd end up back-tracking to get to the familiar places I needed to go.

At some point, I gave up and just walked the whole way, muttering the names of streets I thought I was saying correctly, but couldn't get anyone to understand. *Chan Patan, Chan pa-Tan, JAN-pratan. Siri Mung-kala-jan, Siri Moong-kaleh-jan. Si-ri-mung-koo-la-john.* I comforted myself with my stingy ways. If I didn't pay for a *rot daeng*, I could usually get by on a dollar a day for food and transport. It was possible when you got 40 Baht to the dollar as was the case at the time. I rationed myself three Digestive biscuits and a cup of Nescafe in the morning, the med school cafeteria was cheap and satisfying, for 10 baht you could get a big plate of rice and vegetables, and on the way home I could get sticky rice and curry for 20 Baht, secured in a plastic bag tied up with a rubber band to take home and eat. On a good week, I would splurge on a kilo of sweet tamarind and lie in bed under the air conditioner cracking the pods and chewing on the sweet sticky tart flesh. I spit the clean dark seeds into an aluminum bowl I had borrowed from my landlady. I collected them as if they were pearls for my dowry.

Thailand was generally safe but made me viscerally aware of my social isolation. It was a first experience living by myself, not having an assured social safety net. I was volunteering, I had no employer, no formal relationship with the university, no affiliation with a local organization. If something happened to me, say if I had gotten very sick, I'm not sure what would have happened. If my landlady found me after three days passed out in the bed, who would she have notified? I didn't have access to much money, either cash or credit. I had some flimsy form of traveler's insurance I didn't know how to activate. The people I knew in Thailand were all people I had met after arriving, and they were kind but had no specific obligation or responsibility for me. I had not thought to give anybody, nor had anybody in Thailand asked me for, emergency contact information.

I had a plane ticket to return from Thailand a week before I would walk for graduation. My parents were also flying in to Boston a few days before the ceremony.

The last week I was in Thailand, I began to take a really long time to cross the street. At the corners of the streets I had to cross everyday getting from my rented room to the office, I experienced real dread. I checked myself again and again, to make sure I wasn't looking the wrong way, expecting to see cars or misjudging the speed of the cars approaching. I was sure I was going to get into an accident. So, I stopped on the corner for a long time. I watched the cars from far away get closer and closer and then pass me and then I would look for the next car coming down the road and calculate whether I had time to cross. It was as if I had erased all prior experience of crossing the street and couldn't decide how fast I could cross compared to how much time it would take a car to reach me. I had to recalibrate my judgment every time I crossed. I wanted to see how fast cars at this intersection were traveling at this time of day on this day of the week. And then I adjusted my calculation further so it was very conservative. Then, because I took too long to consider whether I had enough time, a car would get too close and I had to wait for the next opportunity. The shopkeepers at that intersection must have thought I was doing a traffic study, I let so many cars pass before I decided to cross the road.

I remember reflecting on my own irrational behavior at the time. I remember observing that the closer to the day of my departure, the more careful I was being. I knew it was more than just being afraid of getting hit by a car and dying. What I wanted to avoid was the irony of dying just before returning to my friends and family. How much worse would my mother feel if it went down that way. "If she had only come home one week sooner," all her friends would say to my mother at my funeral service. I assumed I would be cremated and sent back to Hawai'i in an urn. There was a certain romance in being shipped back in a coffin, but they would take weeks to locate my parents. Remember, nobody had my emergency contact information! And for that reason, they would turn to cremation because it would be more efficient to store my unclaimed body that way. What a mess. So, I wasn't looking out for my own well-being—no, it was just my strong filial duty to prevent the heartache of my parents which motivated my extreme caution.

I stood on the corner of Niman Haemen Road and Soi 17 watching the cars go by, running the scene from Zeffirelli's *Romeo and Juliet* when the messenger from the friar just misses crossing paths with Romeo because someone is futzing around. Romeo never gets the message about Juliet's poisoning being fake and we all know what happens then. That always killed me, the scene where Romeo's horse leaves just before the messenger arrives. I feel so upset thinking about that scene even now. The tragedy isn't that both Romeo and Juliet die, the tragedy is that these were preventable deaths. There were opportunities to avoid it but due to simple negligence they perished.

And so, in service to my mother, I took my time. I waited.

I let car after car pass. I was going back to the US for my college graduation. Missing that might have actually been tragic to my parents. Somehow, one foot made it in front of the other. I crossed that street, I walked at my college graduation and later that summer I moved to New York.

Before my baby was born, I decided I would make him a quilt. Perhaps this was my symbolic way of providing emotional padding for him. To make up, just a bit, for producing him without a dad.

When my sister had her first baby, it was the first child of the next generation of our family. So, my aunt organized the different branches of the family to each make a quilt square. Then, my aunt sewed everything together and presented the quilt to my sister when the baby was born. I think that's what happens when you have crafty friends too. They make you a present with contributions from different people as a sign of group support and solidarity. We're with you, we are your safety net. Here's proof that we form a web of security around you. If nobody is crafty, someone compiles a baby advice book to share lessons learned, or organizes a meal train so you don't have to cook for the first month.

That doesn't happen if most of your close friends don't live in the same state or don't have kids or if you don't have a workplace or colleagues with whom you spend time in the office. And it's kind of different when you are going to move in with your parents after your baby is born. People think that your family has got it covered and they don't want to step on anyone's toes. For all these reasons, I wasn't expecting to receive a spontaneous show of group support for my baby.

People who have babies on their own often have to be more proactive about organizing group support, I mean the kind that compensates for not having a partner. It's not automatic that people realize you could use that type of help, or it's awkward to offer it, so people don't mention it. But maybe moms going into the newborn phase as single parents need to solicit friends to take shifts living with them just after the baby is born. The way they have to designate the person who's going to be their birthing partner.

Here's an example of something useful to offer a single pregnant person. In addition to contributing his genetic material, my donor granted me "three crazy preggo calls." A preggo call is when you feel upset and usually you would rely on your partner to notice and try to calm you down. It's the time you need to call someone to talk it out, but you feel foolish reaching out to people because what you're going to say requires the listener to practice non-judging, unconditional loving. And also, you want the security that after the crazy call, the listener won't avoid contact with you forever after. My donor said "crazy preggo call" privileges could be redeemed at any time of day, for any situation I required, because everyone knows crazy preggo time happens at inconvenient times of the day. I didn't end up using any preggo calls (until after the birth), but it felt nice to have them as part of my safety net.

I had never made a quilt before, but the idea held great appeal for me. It hit all my buttons. I never could draw, but I longed to be artistic. I liked the idea of piecing together small repeating geometric shapes that could result in a larger pattern with some calculation and planning. Quilting involves geometric rules, an indoor setting, and rewards the thriftiness of using scrap materials. I was made for quilting. I was already operating in the mode of doing things for myself, I had the time and inclination, and this was something I wanted for my baby.

I chose the pattern: a series of squares, each composed of diagonal strips, which are then sewn together to form large diamonds. It is called the God's Eye pattern. It reminded me of my Summer Fun days in the early 80s, where I learned to make God's Eyes out of yarn and popsicle sticks. You glue two sticks into a cross and wrap the yarn between the sticks, over and under, over and under, over and under. It could take 20 minutes, if you were being careful and laying the yarn close together. You could change the color of the yarn two or three times during the weaving to make it really look like an eye: the pupil, the iris, the sclera, etc. Making one was peaceful and satisfying like good hippie crafts should be. I hadn't done one since those Summer Fun days, but I couldn't wait for the day when my kid would be making them too. Choosing the God's Eye for my quilt project felt perfect.

I also liked the idea that the eye belonged to God, but there wasn't just one eye or a pair of eyes, the finished quilt would have a bunch of eyes. So that made it not so much a Judeo-Christian God's eye, and more like a Greek or Hindu gods' eyes thing. Possibly a multi-headed god or a team of gods. As I mentioned before, I don't believe in God, but I don't mind invoking God's power for others, in case I'm wrong. A real god wouldn't let the atheism of the mother penalize the child. It wouldn't hurt to have some higher power looking over my baby in case I died in childbirth or got struck by a bus a few years later.

I wanted this quilt to have vibrant red/pink pupils surrounded by blue/purple irises. That informed the color palette of the scraps I would use. This quilt was not going to be in gentle pastels, it had to radiate some kind of force field of good vibes protecting my baby. It needed strong colors.

I announced my quilting project in an email to a group of friends and family, some in faraway places. These were people I didn't see regularly, but were all people I wanted to keep in my life, would want my kid to meet and to get to know someday. I asked these people to send some fabric they had already, from something old that they had worn or was around their house. It was meant to be a non-creepy way to get good friend juju to my baby from the get-go. I thought it was better than asking people to send snips of their hair for a voodoo doll or for stuffing into a weird talisman my baby could wear around his neck.

Part of the joy of quilting is piecing together disparate pieces to see how it will look all sewn together. In the God's Eye pattern, the center diagonal stripe of each square acts as the anchor of the design. I used the same fabric in every square because that is what connects to form the bigger pattern of diamonds of the quilt, god's eyeliner, so to speak. I cut these center strips from a blue-gray ikat silk I had bought during that first foray into public health in Thailand. It was kind of an old lady piece of silk, the colors a bit muted, the pattern minute and serious. It was old, sewn into a sarong, soft and strong, it had been worn many times before I had ever owned it. When I got back from Thailand I had given it to my sister. But because of the old lady look and they weren't really her colors she hadn't worn it much and after a few years I had borrowed it back.

Different friends began sending in their pieces of cloth. One friend in Seattle sent a piece of flannel from her favorite pajamas, light blue with yellow and white and navy bubbles. The gift of sweet dreams. My cousin sent a Winnie-the-Pooh plaid fabric she had used to sew curtains for the window in her girls' nursery. Gentle breezes, a smackeral of honey. Another friend sent a purple butterfly dress her daughter had just outgrown in soft, soft Indian cotton. The kind of cotton you're happy to wear when the Delhi monsoon is late, it's 105 degrees outside and the power's been cut. Another friend had sent a piece of fabric she had gotten while living in Botswana. It had a serious navy and white diamond calico print. It came stiff and new and smooth, the logo of three cat faces printed cleanly on the back. It was from Da Gama Textiles, the original maker of South African indigo cotton *shwe shwe*. A fittingly reappropriated product of colonialism. My quilting friend sent an assortment of pieces leftover from her own projects. She said she sent her brightest blues. My crafty aunt contributed some clown prints from the seventies she had used in blankets for her kids and leftover cotton from house dresses she had made for my grandmother when my grandmother couldn't see well enough to thread the needle on her machine anymore.

I had accumulated a big collection of dress material myself: pieces of batik I had gotten as presents on work trips: both presents from others, and presents to myself; leftover Hawaiian prints from the Christmas I had made reusable sandwich bags as presents, a phase in my life when I thought it was a good use of my time to make reusable sandwich bags. The bright reds I needed for the center of the God's Eyes came from a signature swing dress in a mod floral I had made for myself in high school. I dug through my mother's scrap bag and found the pieces of Marimekko fabric she had hunted for in remnant piles at dry goods stores when I was in middle school because buying off the bolt was too expensive. With those small pieces, a quarter yard or less, she would make pillows for the sofa and school bags for me and my sister. Somewhere in my scrap bag, there was a 1940s cherry printed seersucker from the now demented Aunty Yung.

I spent many evenings in Hilo cutting my strips, sewing them together, trimming them square and composing the most pleasing arrangement of God's Eyes. The thunder of the sewing machine drowned out the sound of rain on the tin roof and coqui frogs trying to get laid in the foliage. (Another group that doesn't need online dating in

Hilo.) I found constructing the quilt to be addictive, the satisfaction of completing each square, then building each row, the high as each eye came into view. I patted my belly thoughtfully; picked the stray threads and trimmed edges off the floor, and reconsidered the arrangement of squares. Meditative, absorbing. The comfort of this quilt was that it was unconventional: it wasn't meant to line up exactly, the strips were intended to be varying width, and beyond lining up the central strip and the color of the eye centers, nothing else had to match. It was even better the more contrast there was between the strips of the adjacent squares. It was a Crazy Gods' Eyes quilt, if that's a thing.

It was a quilt that stitched together person, place, and time, and also a world of experiences, many that weren't even mine. "Person, Place and Time" are the epidemiologists' holy trinity. Each is key to describing and understanding an unfolding epidemic. These details tell the epidemiologist how to take in what's happening, predict the trajectory and know what's needed to control the situation.

I finished my quilt a month or so before my baby was due. For the backing I found a piece of upholstery fabric. It featured blue chinoiserie-styled dog-lions frolicking with peonies on a terracotta ground. The material was something I had picked up in Thailand more recently, when I first became an independent consultant. It was sturdy but the material had a polished finish that made it cool to the touch. I thought it would be nice for my baby to lie on in the Indian Summer months following his birth.

Actually, another reason I had used it as the backing was that it was printed by the House of Jim Thompson. Mister Jim Thompson was the white guy who revitalized the silk export industry in Thailand and was also an OSS agent, in the days before the CIA. He disappeared mysteriously in a Malaysian jungle in the late 60s. That little bit of intrigue in the background, the unknown whereabouts of a white male figure, seemed kind of apropos. Besides, it was the perfect size to attach to my pieced squares.

Attaching the backing was the last step. I thought it seemed straightforward. Except if you're an inexperienced quilter and don't always measure, it's not easy to pin something kind of crazy and made imperfectly to a solid stable backing. The quilt ended up lumpy and not very square. It was thick and not as large as I intended. It was big enough to be a pad my baby could lie on for the first few months when he couldn't yet turn over. After that, regarding its utility as baby protection, we'd have to see. I was okay with that. The pattern was random and pleasing, it had juju, it gave me joy to make, and that was all by design.

CHOKING

AT 32 WEEKS, I MOVED from Hilo to Honolulu, and transferred myself to another obstetrician's practice on Oahu. My Honolulu OB was a bit younger than me, but Cantonese, born and raised in Hawai'i, like me. Maybe if I had gone to med school, I would have had a life similar to hers. That's what I thought when I met her at my first appointment in Honolulu. She was wearing hospital scrubs and a white lab coat that day. And the same when I saw her about a month later for the next appointment. But the appointment after that ended up getting rescheduled. Turns out, my OB was in labor, so the nurse had to schedule me to see her practice partner instead. Whaaat?!? I had no clue that she was pregnant. And the amazing thing was not just the power of a white lab coat to conceal, but only three weeks after she gave birth, she was right back in the office taking appointments as if she had not just brought another human being into the world. At that point, I concluded that even if I had gone to med school, I would not have led a life similar to hers.

It was getting late in the game. On my first visit, she started asking questions about my birth plan.

"Have you taken a birth class?" I shook my head. "It could be helpful," she said. "They can answer your questions, like which entrance at the hospital if you arrive ready to deliver? Where to pay? What options are offered at the hospital that can be included in your birth plan?"

My OB also had a sign in every exam room in her office that says, "We try to accommodate your wishes as specified in your birth plan as much as possible, but we may not always be able to honor these requests in the interests of safety for you or your child. All elements of patients' birth plans must be discussed with your doctor more than one month before your expected due date to be considered."

It struck me as funny that they had to post these signs. If a patient really got irate because they didn't get the experience they wanted, would remembering that they saw a sign on a wall calm them down? Did the doctor expect to point to the sign if their patients lodged a complaint or expressed disappointment? I thought maybe it was a reminder that the OB should feel empowered to say, "Yeah, bringing your cat into the delivery room is not a safe practice and cannot be part of the plan." Sort of like those employee hand washing signs in restaurant bathrooms.

"Yes." Okay, those were good questions. "I will definitely sign up for a class," I gulped.

That was the kind of class I needed to take, the kind that answers questions I had not thought to ask. I had been planning to arrive at the emergency room when my labor started, isn't that what they did on TV? And this issue of payment, it didn't occur to me that someone would be asking me to give them a credit card at the hospital. Don't they just bill your insurance? They don't show that part on TV. Then there was the birth plan. Um. Get the baby out. Do it safely. Do it quickly. Don't wreck anything unnecessarily.

Golden rule. Treat my vagina as you would your own. What else do you have to specify?

Then again, I am the kind of person who goes shopping for a home appliance or a car and invariably gets the mid-priced model from a large retailer. No customization, no special features. I want it to work. I want to be able to return it. I don't want to spend a lot of money. Would decision-making about my birth plan be so different? If somebody, say my OB, asked me what I wanted, I would say, "What do you recommend?" And I hoped they would tell me what was necessary for a statistically probable good outcome, i.e. a normal delivery.

As my doctor recommended, I signed myself up for a birthing class and a tour of the hospital. The online registration form for the class posed the first good question I encountered, "Who was going to accompany me to class?" A birthing class is not for pregnant ladies, it is for birthing couples. "Who are you going to bring to class," really means, "Who do you expect to be at the delivery with you." Some hospitals call this your birthing partner. Some refer to this person as your birth attendant. The default answer is the father of your child, or to be inclusive, your "life partner." I didn't have one of those, but—hah! this was one part of my birth plan that I had already thought about. (I was acing this thing.)

I wanted my sister to be with me when I delivered. Mostly, I wanted her to be around to drive me to the hospital. My mother gets nervous about being late and encountering traffic, she wouldn't want to drive. But my dad is a notoriously slow mover (gathering keys, changing his shirt, sauntering to the car, driving in the far-right lane).

I imagined sitting in the back of a car during labor, my father at the wheel and my mother next to him feeling nervous. Soon she would channel her anxiety into yelling at my father, the driver. My father's response to a confrontational situation is not fight or flight, it's freeze. I call it Hedgehog Mind. He doesn't literally roll into a ball, but mentally plays dead. Those are not the qualities of a driver that get you swiftly to a hospital.

My mother might be a bird of prey perched in the passenger seat, her eyes turning yellow as she sees a juicy rodent become a ball of impenetrable spikes. She would start yelling some more. Because one thing you learn from living with a hedgehog for forty years, you don't get used to it, it just more efficiently pushes your buttons. It makes you shriek more. I did some calculations and concluded that relying on my parents to drive me to the hospital would constitute a preventable unattended birth in a vehicle. So even though my sister lived in New Jersey, it might be faster if she flew in to take me to the hospital. Actually, we planned for her to come in a week before my due date. Not an easy thing for her to do. She had her life, including two kids. At least she was a teacher and had the summer off. But she certainly couldn't come six weeks early just to take a birthing class with me. So I signed my mom up. She would come to the class. It couldn't hurt, after all she was my birth attendant understudy.

The first Saturday, the class started with everyone going around the room introducing themselves. The one giving birth is empowered to take the lead.

"Hi I'm Jolene and this is my husband Andy, this is our second child. We're due in December."

"Hello everyone, I'm Tricia."

"And I'm Derrick."

"We're having a girl. And we're due in August." Smiling look at each other, raised eyebrows in mutual excitement and trepidation. Smile again. "Oh, this is our first baby."

And then it was my turn. "Hi, I'm Virginia." Pause. "Um, this is my first baby." Pause. "Oh, It's due in August too." Smile at Tricia and Derrick in a moment of connection. "I'm here with my mom."

Pause. Everyone else looked like they came with their partner. Should I identify myself as a single mom? Was I even a mom yet? Should I mention that I had a donor? To a room of people I'd never met before, it seemed like too much information. But did they think the baby daddy wasn't with me, because I had just gotten knocked up, or we had split up already? I tried to think of other scenarios for coming to the class without the baby daddy. I could be a military wife. Maybe my husband was active duty and maybe that's the reason that he was not in class. I was a bit older than a typical military wife. Would people find military wife to be a plausible explanation? Then I had a moment of clarity and stopped myself. Why do I need to explain myself to anyone? Then came another clarifying thought, nobody cares what my situation is. People are just minding their own business, not speculating about mine.

The resolution on my face must have signaled to the next couple that I was done and not going to say anymore.

"Hey, we're Sherry and—"

"Oh, sorry," I interrupted, "I meant to say, this is my mother. Oh, wait, I already said that, Sorry, Sherry, okay, go ahead. Sorry. Sorry." *Arghhh*. It was official. I was the class weirdo.

I felt sensitive because really a birthing class is geared toward making couples closer as they go prime time in this life-changing experience. That's what the instructor, Sue, explained, "This class is not only about the physical process of how to bring new life into the world. A positive and successful birthing experience also prepares you for how you as a couple will deal with each other as you go through the process of raising a child."

The other couples looked at each other lovingly. Some got into cuddle position. I looked at my mother. She looked nervous. As if she was expecting this to be a cooking class and then when she arrived someone told her she would be delivering a baby instead. She acted as if she had not herself gone through childbirth twice before. She looked like she was looking for someone to yell at if my birthing experience didn't go well.

Sue wore a nametag that indicated she was a nurse. She was a woman in her early 60s wearing a purple T-shirt and with a home sewn patchwork vest, some practical long khaki shorts, long socks, practical shoes. She had neat iron-gray curls in a tidy bob. She reminded me of the kind of person who runs girl scout camps, the kind of adult comfortable in a scouting uniform. She picked up on some of the feel-good energy in the room, and got animated as she continued with her introduction.

"We're going to ask questions! Dads, listen up! We're going to ask 'what does it mean to be supportive?'" She raised her eyebrows and looked knowingly around at the men in the room. "I'm talking to you, Dad." She paused in front of one couple. "Dads, you are in a support role, you are not giving birth. Am I right, Moms? So, this means we're going to talk about how you can observe what Mom is experiencing, let her take the lead in how to handle the discomfort of labor and then support her in that process. Okay?"

That sounded good to me. I wondered if my mom understood that when Sue said, "Dads" that she was part of that group. I hoped she wasn't thinking she was the "Mom" experiencing discomfort and who should take the lead in telling others what to do about it.

I hoped she was clear about Sue's pep talk, so she could go through the same spiel with my sister. I should give my mom more credit, but she is the type of person who watches an Agatha Christie movie with you and then at the end, after the whole big reveal, says, "I don't get it."

My mother is a smart person, but gets impatient. If she loses the plot at the beginning, then she just gives up on tracking how the whole thing is going to turn out. Then when you explain the whole convoluted plot she shrugs her shoulders as if to say, "Well that wasn't really worth trying to follow anyway."

It wasn't quite a murder mystery, but there were a lot of things about the plot of my birth story that she might have given up trying to understand. She was just waiting for the baby to pop out, to find out "who dunnit," then she would try to get some satisfaction out of the whole thing. She didn't really need to know how it all fit together. Trying to catch her up in the middle just wasn't worth the trouble.

"I'm going to warn you, *Dads*, by the end there's probably going to be some yelling and a lot of discomfort and maybe some anger. Not in class, hopefully." Nervous laughter from the group. Was she looking at my mother? "I'm talking about during the birth now. What is your job, Dads? ... Support! Your job is NOT to make YOUR OWN discomfort stop, right?" Knowing pause from Sue, she made eye contact with a number of Dads. "Ok, we'll talk more about this later. I just want to clarify what we're here for."

Throughout the class, all this emphasis on cultivating a healthy relationship with your parenting partner made me feel the absence of a real partner in this process sharply. The birthing exercises Sue led us through also made me wonder how comforting a birth attendant my sister or mother would make.

We had to put a clothespin on our ears to manifest some pain and then lean on our partners who physically supported our bodies, then helped us to breathe deeply and gave back massages to get us through the discomfort. Most of the other women's partners were built like Lazy Boy recliners. My sister and my mother are both thin women who I thought would collapse under the weight of my fully pregnant self. It was like trying to cuddle with a kitchen stool.

On the other hand, I had the advantage that my birthing partner had actually gone through labor and didn't need to put a clothespin on her ear to develop empathy for what I

Virginia Loo

would be going through. Not only had she had two babies, my sister had two babies without epidurals! I began to think that made us the best theoretical birthing "couple" in the class.

The next thought I had was *Wait, my birthing partner had two babies without epidurals?* My birthing partner was crazy.

At some point, we covered epidurals in the class. All the "Moms" (not my mom, who was hanging out with the "Dads") had to stand up and arrange themselves along a spectrum of those insisting on having a completely natural birth and those really, seriously wanting an epidural. The ends of the spectrum could be described as: those who were looking forward to the birthing process as an amazing experience and not wanting to miss any part of it, and those who were dreading the delivery and all the pain.

I was three quarters along the spectrum towards "The anesthesiologist will be the most important person at my delivery."

Maybe I wasn't dreading a painful delivery so much. I was dreading what seemed like it would be such an emotionally intense moment. I remembered hearing a male friend describe the incredible moment of being in the delivery room with his wife during the birth of their first child. "It was amazing! Laura was so beautiful. She was so strong during the whole thing. When the pain came, she just breathed through it and stayed calm. We never felt so close to each other as when she was going through labor. And then when you see your child. Incredible! It was just the most—unbelievable moment to have together. I didn't know it was going to be that way."

A moment shared with a life partner. Well, that wasn't going to be my experience. Who was I going to look at and cry with when this baby came out? Was it going to be the most beautiful moment in my life and would I witness it alone?

During the tour of the birthing facility, I could see this campaign to promote birth as magical and fantastic everywhere I looked. The painted butterflies and woodland animals whispering sweet thoughts to each other on the walls. The soft pink faux tapestry upholstery pull-out sleeper chairs made for dads to curl up next to their exhausted but glowing partner. The softly breathing cocooned newborn's bassinet in a dimly lit corner of the room. As we tiptoed through these sacred spaces, I understood that these rooms served as a transitional womb for a new family. The next day, this newly configured organism would emerge into the daylight, go to billing and hand over their credit card, and then get discharged into the world. As I made my way down the corridor of birthing rooms, I thought I could hear a low primordial groan, a last push as a nuclear family covered in a goo of emotion and adrenaline gushed out of the hospital.

Then I had another idea, even more disturbing than having no one to go to the emotional Mt. Everest of my life with. What if I *didn't* experience much feeling when I gave birth? Maybe the truth was, I was someone lacking a deep, loamy emotional life. Was I going to experience giving birth with no deeper satisfaction than I had while receiving delivery of a brand-new washer and dryer?

Up to that point, the only live birth I had witnessed had been more than fifteen years earlier in Thailand. One of my assignments during the time I spent working on the HIV clinical trial was visiting potential study hospitals to assess their interest in the project and gather information about their patient population. I had been, until a month before, a college student. I hadn't been in a position to be interviewing anyone. I wore my best v-neck t-shirt and sandals instead of flip flops to the meet these heads of hospital departments. I tried my best to appear professional and to represent my institution.

Well.

I didn't fool anyone. They took one look at me when I arrived at the hospital and knew exactly how I fit into this whole research study hierarchy. I was a student from Harvard, so I must be smart and a good worker, or potentially have very rich parents. I was working for a Harvard professor with whom they wanted to be affiliated. They humored me, they gave me the information that I needed to relay back to the principal investigator, and then they treated me like their teenage daughters. They took me to their homes; they fed me ice cream with durian. They asked me about my own parents. They told me to work hard and not to walk around the city by myself at night.

While visiting one site, the head of obstetrics was called to a delivery while I was interviewing her. She asked casually, "Would you like to see how we do it?"

And I said, "Yes. That would be great."

She meant, would I like to observe their labor and delivery practices to assess whether their protocols would be compatible with the study. And I meant, yes, I would like to witness how humans birth their young.

I followed the OB down the hall to the waiting woman.

Boy, was she ready to deliver.

I wondered, was there some kind of etiquette to the process of observing another person's birth? Or more accurately, observing another person give birth?

I had been thinking of myself as a guest at a wedding, brought by a friend of the family because you are visiting from another country the weekend of the wedding and you have never attended this type of cultural event. I'd been in that situation a couple of times and it always surprised me how willing the main participants in the event, say the father of the bride, are to take the time to explain to their uninvited guest all the rituals involved and the symbolism and the history. How willing they are to treat the bride and groom as a cultural display, instead of the stars of their special day. That says something about those types of weddings, which are more about the establishing a new branch of a family than about two people declaring eternal love to each other. But attending a wedding and watching someone give birth are not the same thing. I had not thought through the ethics of the situation.

I did as I was told and planned to be deeply observant without being disruptive or rude. Someone deposited me in the corner of the operating theater where the heavily breathing pregnant woman was struggling into stirrups. I may have been given a mask, but she certainly wasn't told who I was, nor asked if I could observe. The room was much larger than the table she was lying on.

There was a moment when everyone had left the room to retrieve something or other, and besides me, she was alone in the middle of the room.

She may not have processed that I was there. I acted as if I wasn't there. Under the fluorescent lights she looked green, the same color as the gown she wore, the surgical sheet that had been pulled over her abdomen and draped over her knees. The room was stark, but it wasn't a bad place. It was clean: concrete floors, plaster walls painted ice blue, accented with water stains and WHO posters instructing on the use of personal protective equipment, no fantasy talking woodland animals on the walls there. The only disturbing thing was a panel of overloaded electrical sockets, flanked by a shrill, tan plastic desk phone screwed to the wall.

Then there was a lot of loud talking in the hallway and two nurses came in wheeling a cart of birthing tools followed by the doctor. The birth began.

I was not prepared. I had never seen anything like it before. Not even on video. It was bloody, and there was agony, and I almost passed out, standing in the corner. I had to sneak out and sit down on a plastic stool near the desk where the nurses did their paperwork, breathing quietly to myself until I could see clearly again. I couldn't imagine what the woman giving birth was feeling. But her experience was treated as normal. Everything went according to plan. She got her baby. She went home.

But she did not look like she had an epiphany. Her partner did not attend the birth. They did not become one as part of an amazing birthing experience. And they probably did fine as parents of their kids.

At any rate I decided that my delivery was going to be emotionally no frills. That was my birth plan. Stay focused on outcomes. What was I going to feel or not feel? Who knew? Luckily, my sister and I were close, but we weren't sentimental with each other. She would follow my lead on how verklempt to get. I was ready to have a standard, regular, everyday spontaneous vaginal delivery. Just like that Thai lady who had been so generous to share her birth experience. Bring it on.

Except you should know that I am a choker.

I came to terms with this in the eighth grade when I started taking serious tennis lessons from a teacher who coached state high school champions.

I learned a lot from those tennis lessons.

First off was irony. My coach trained state champions that went to fancy private schools on public high school tennis courts she used for free.

Secondly, I learned about cheating the system and co-opting children to help you do that. She wasn't supposed to use public courts to give private lessons. If anybody asked, we were told to say she was just volunteering to coach us. Her two sons would push us through rallies while she yelled at us from the sideline. "Pick up your lazy butts. Let's go!

Let's go!"

We had to pay her for each session, so some time during the lesson we had to make our way to a bench on the sidelines and shove an envelope of cash into her purse. We all did it, every lesson, but we all pretended we didn't. It was like an unspoken rule that we weren't supposed to talk about how we actually paid for our lessons. Once, there was an incident when someone from the county dropped by. And then for some reason lessons were canceled for about three weeks. And then they started up again as usual, and we all showed up with our lazy butts, cash in an envelope tucked into a purse behind a garbage can on one side of the court.

After school twice a week, I caught a ride to group tennis lessons with other wannabe champions who went to my school. On Saturdays I did one-on-one lessons. And through these lessons I developed a pretty decent two-handed backhand. It was stinging actually. I was a back court specialist. And I loved a long rally.

But then my teacher kept insisting I sign up for tournaments, because the point of playing tennis was to win games, not hit balls. The first tournament I was in, I wore a pair of new white shorts, I put on a brand-new grip tape. But in the first round, I got beaten by Valerie Ching, a girl whose only weapons were hustle and a moon ball that always fell in.

She didn't win, I choked. I saw that high ball come over the net and take a huge bounce and I'd try to spin it back in a punishing shot cross court, but it went wild, flying over the line. The next time a ball came toward my end of the court a million doubts would enter my head and I whiffed the ball.

Valerie was on to something, and she did it over and over while I showed her a whole variety of ways not to get the ball back in the court. I began to dread the very ball I used to love seeing coming over the net.

That's the difference between choking and panic. Panic is failing because you can't think; Choking is when you fail because you think too much. I read that distinction in a New Yorker article by Malcolm Gladwell, *The Art of Failure* (2000). An article written a few months after his first book *The Tipping Point* was published. The article starts off by analyzing the epitome of choking in sports made famous by Jana Novotna at the Wimbledon championships in 1993. I related to that first paragraph so strongly. But I was not Jana. When I lost to Queen Valerie of the Moonballs, there was no kind Duchess of Kent to tell me, "I know one day you will win it, don't worry."

During prime time of any kind, my heart starts pounding, my face gets red, and I begin to sweat. Because when you are a choker, you think about being a choker, and know that you're going to choke. When I choke, I just can't bear to find out that I'm going to lose. Even if there's a good chance that I have the preparation or the skills, that it will be a good outcome, I entertain the non-zero possibility of failure. The what-ifs become a barrage of moon balls that a competent person could send back, but in my chock-full-of-choking-state-of-mind, I miss completely. When I visualize what future failure looks like, or just replay past ones in a loop, I think to myself, let me just save the effort, pre-empt the expectation, spare myself the agony, why wait to see what is going to happen. And I give up.

I'll give you another example, involving the snows of Kilimanjaro. If you're ever in Tanzania and you look up at it, you will see global warming is real. The snow up there, it's disappearing. "If you don't go to see it soon, then there will be nothing to see later." That's what my friend told me in 2008, to convince me to climb Mt. Kilimanjaro with her.

She had a friend who ran a tour company escorting tourists on these kinds of treks. There would be porters carrying all the gear, there would be a bathroom tent, a shower tent, a dining room tent and a cook. All I had to do was get my butt up the mountain. We would take one of the long easier routes to acclimate, what could make the close-to-never-more-in-a-lifetime experience easier?

The first five days, we gradually ascended the foothills. Our bodies acclimated to the altitude, and the guides coach you in a mantra of *pole-pole*, slow and steady. One woman in our group was a juggernaut of a trekker, and the guides cautioned her drive. They pointed to me and the pace I kept as a good example. I was the poster child of *pole-pole*. So far, so good. We were nearing the top, but our training was paying off, we were ready. Then at dawn between the end of Day 6 and the beginning of Day 7, halfway through the last leg to reach the summit, I had to stop. We had awoken at midnight to start the sunrise hike to the top. We had joined a huge queue of trekkers and guides, snaking up the mountain. At this point, the mountain top looks like a gray pile of gravel. My boots sunk deep into scree if I stepped off the narrow trail of packed ground made by the many, many trekkers that came before me.

I was moving very slowly; I felt the altitude and the cold. Suddenly, I was feeling incredibly sleepy. So sleepy I had to keep sitting down even though there was a long trail of other hikers behind us. We couched on the side to let the unending line of people pass. I kept babbling in a drunken way to the guide. I was doing *pole-pole*, slow and steady, just like they coached us. But really, I just wanted to lie down. I wanted to spread out my arms and legs and make an angel out of small dusty rocks, say my prayers and go to sleep. I stopped and sat, then rallied to stand up and go another fifty feet before sitting down again. Pole-pole, just like they said. I can do it. But I'm so sleepy. And then I announced it outright. "I'm done." I was through, it had been very nice, thank you for the experience, but I was ready to go back down.

The guide looked at me in dismay, not wanting to hear me. "Madame, *never* in the history of the company, Madame, has a guest not finished getting up the mountain. Never." He looked at me pleadingly. "I can help you Madame, you have made it this far. I cannot let you stop." He was not my Duchess of Kent, embracing me and my defeat, encouraging me to try again someday. In retrospect, I realize the guide's insistence that I keep going was not for my benefit or to give me satisfaction in getting my money's worth. It wasn't fear that when the oxygen returned to my blood that I would accuse him of malpractice, not being able to get me to the top. It was not even a matter of personal pride that the guides could lead the infirm and the aged up successfully. It was mostly just bad business to have to admit that on occasion an able-bodied youngish guest (I was 34 at the time) had not made it to the top.

The guide insisted again that I let him drag me up the mountain no matter what. For that moment on the side of the mountain, I thought I should rally for the men who had lugged my ridiculously large duffle bag of stuff for me, carried a rubber bladder full of water and heated it over a fire to provide a hot shower experience at the end of every day, carted a head of cauliflower and a box of Velveeta up the mountain to make a comforting cheesy noodle casserole the night before. These men who slept in the open and drank only one small bottle of water a day. I owed it to them. I felt a renewed commitment to get up the hill for their sake surging within me. I stood up. Then a tide of sleepiness hit me sideways again and by instinct me and my trekking poles began skiing down the scree toward camp as

I had seen those who finished the trek earlier that morning do so effortlessly and gracefully. At least I didn't have to be carried down the mountain by my guide, I comforted myself.

I've gotten to the point of self-soothing that I can rationalize most bouts of choking. I am my own Duchess of Kent.

I tell myself it's not failure, it's just not my time. I tell myself I am the kind of person who gives it my all—within reason. I love moderation, so to give it "my all," is more like 90%. I cherish the idea of reserve, having contingency, maintaining a margin of error, ensuring a cushion. It goes along with the assessment of risk and being acutely aware of a preventable death, even more so if it is my own. That is why I'm a natural public health professional.

The unkind way to say it is, I'm a choker, but I look at it as focusing on a different outcome: getting 90% of the way up the summit and making sure I could make it down the mountain.

Can I tell you that when you are pregnant, being prepped at the hospital to go through a regular vaginal delivery, it feels like sitting in the locker room before stepping on the court for a Wimbledon final?

Am I ready? Have I trained enough? Do I need to stretch? Where is my coach?

In the end, things did not go exactly as planned.

I had been sure I was going to deliver early. I had been dilated three and a half centimeters for the last three weeks. I worried that my sister wouldn't make it in time. I asked her to leave the kids with her husband and come a few days earlier than scheduled.

But then we waited. We walked up and down the hill where my parents live trying to get my labor started. But we just waited some more. Things were not going completely as planned. So my doctor scheduled me for induction. I was already one week overdue by that morning.

I checked into the hospital at 8 in the morning and then pumped some Pitocin into my system to jumpstart some contractions. The monitor they hooked to me showed the contractions coming but I didn't really feel them when they were at their peak, something was off.

It wasn't anything like what I was taught in that birthing class. In the third or fourth session, Sue had simulated the labor experience using a blue striped knitted uterus with a baby doll inside. During this part of the class, Sue's voice oozed, warm and soothing. I was mesmerized as she described the process of active labor. She held the faux uterus in front of her and played it like it was a magic bag pipe. She squeezed it rhythmically and demonstrated the steady downward progression of the plastic baby with each contraction, until it emerged in full and she kissed it on the top of the head to signal that the birth was complete and all was well.

That experience was as removed as how I felt on the Pitocin. I watched the monitor tell me when the contraction was at its peak, but didn't feel pinched and contorted until what was supposed to be the downstroke. Something was wrong with my bagpipes.

In addition, a few days before my induction, my sister had admitted that she was almost three months pregnant and feeling extremely gaseous. She already suffered from terrible heartburn. At the hospital, she tried to coach me through the contractions while not getting sick all over the place.

Without compunction, I got my epidural as soon as it was offered. Then they upped the Pitocin to see if that would help and we went another 12 hours. By this time, it was near midnight. I was at a teaching hospital and so more than twelve hours of laboring in the hospital meant that I experienced several rounds of students and interns and I guess residents too, trying out their newly learned techniques on me. When you first get to the hospital, they do ask you if you are okay with it. At that point, I was feeling fresh and ready to go. I said, "Sure."

I thought I was supporting higher education. But it turned out to be a bit like donating your body to science, except you're not dead yet. I was trying to push a live human being out of myself, but now with the pressure of witnesses, I tried to do it pleasantly, gracefully, smiling. The interns stuck their hands in me and checked my cervix while a crowd of med students watched intently. When they figured out I hadn't progressed since the last check three hours ago, they called the attending, to check again to see if the intern did it right. The nurse who is standing behind the crowd, slowly shakes her head, because she knows he did not do it right. Then the attending comes and confirms, it's true I haven't progressed, by his calculations I'd even regressed a bit.

Regressed! Meaning my baby has started ascending. Is that possible? I wanted there to be a comforting Duchess of Womb in there to say, "I know you will be born one day, don't worry." Maybe it was just not his time. But then the attending suggested that "they" break my water to help things move along. Unlike the other procedures, breaking my water could only be done by one lucky medical trainee. My best hope was that the attending wanted to demonstrate the procedure with skill to the rest.

Sure, why not? While you all are here, demonstrate something else. What's the point of delivering in a teaching hospital if you can't provide an interesting educational experience? Before I could think much more about it, somebody, I don't remember who, hopefully the attending, stuck another implement in me to nick my womb while the crowd held their breath. But then nothing perceptible descended. So, they let me get some sleep and the nurse woke me up every hour to turn me on to my other side. I could hear my sister lying in the reclining chair next to me, quietly groaning in her sleep from the acid reflux.

So, by that time it was 8:30 am the next morning. Mt. Kilimanjaro comes to mind. My OB arrived to do rounds and she saw I hadn't progressed, she asked me the question, laid it all out for me and waited for my answer.

"The baby is fine, we could probably do this for another 12 hours, and see what happens. If the baby starts to get distressed, we would do a C-section, but we can keep going like this until that happens. The other option would be to just do the C-section now. The whole thing will take about 45 minutes. What would you like to do?"

The question was unexpected. I had been expecting to do a vaginal delivery the whole time. I was prepared. I had spent six weekends in a row practicing various breathing techniques, I had practiced rhythmic breathing with a clothespin on my ear to see if I could stand it. And despite being a self-aware choker, I was all in for this spontaneous vaginal delivery. I had read all the medical literature, it was better for the baby, it was better for me, which ultimately meant better for the baby.

All those terrible statistics about elective C-sections in the US, as a public health professional, how could I choose otherwise. But now, my very sensible, hard-core OB, probably five years younger than me, who eight weeks earlier had popped out a baby herself, then three weeks later came back to work looking like that was a normal thing to do, was offering me an opportunity to choose a very legitimate C-section. I could see my sister standing bravely by the side of my bed, ready to support whatever decision I made, looking concerned about the hard choice presented to me. But it was so easy, choosing the C-section, just like pivoting and skiing down a mountain of scree.

Once I made the decision, it went so quickly. They put my sister in some scrubs covered in a gown, they put on a cap and a mask. She looked like she was going to decontaminate a biohazard site. That site being my womb. They got me on the table and wheeled me into the room. And they put a curtain over my middle so I couldn't see what was happening. *Good decision*, I thought. *That's probably standard with a C-section and that's a good decision.*

They gave me more anesthesia, but I was still supposed to be awake. By this time, I was feeling really sleepy, I just wanted to close my eyes. I was fighting hard to stay awake because it seemed a shame to miss the birth of your own baby. There was stuff going on in/on my abdomen, I could feel pressure and some pulling but it was like I was simultaneously underwater, sleepy and completely numb from the bottom down. And then what woke me up was my OB saying, "Oh my god, this baby is humongous!"

I looked up at my sister and she was looking over the curtain and looked like she was going to pass out. I wanted to say with my eyes, the only thing I felt capable of moving, I know how you feel. But actually, I probably had no idea of how she felt. This woman, my sister, who had two children without an epidural, someone who had been very present for the birth of her two children, and she looked like she was going to faint.

Maybe she was thinking that in about six months she might have to push out a similarly large baby out herself, except vaginally without pain killers, and that combined with some bad hospital vending machine coffee, made her feel ill. Later, she said she wished they had pulled the curtain a lot higher so that she did not have to see the incision and the removal of the baby. "That was...a lot!" she said. She didn't expect it to happen like that. She had almost lost it in the delivery room.

I worried: maybe there was something about my baby in particular that was unsettling. The fact that my doctor expressed uncensored surprise about the shape of my baby—huge!—alarmed me. Wasn't she in charge? Wasn't she keeping track of all this?

Was he also an alien, was he green? What was behind that curtain?

But then they cleaned him up and brought him over and he was perfect. Plump and pink and bright alert eyes. And while I was admiring my baby but not really able to hold him because they were stitching me up, I did feel out of body and unreal. I don't even remember how long I got to look at him, but they wheeled him away and then I was really sleepy, and they took me away to rest and I did fall asleep and woke up a little later, and they said to rest and in about two hours they check to see if there are no more large chunks of your body dislodging and sluicing out.

They wheeled me in a bed to my room. It looked empty and quiet as if someone had recently died in there and things have been specially sterilized physically and spiritually. I felt lonely because I was there by myself. I was supposed to be resting. Undisturbed. It felt empty because my baby was not there with me, yet. I wanted the space to fill, to be taken up by this person who is now the one I love the most in all the world. And it also felt odd to love someone I hadn't really met yet. I wanted to see him. And at the same time, I was terrified to be left alone with him. I felt like everything below my neck was paralyzed. Really, I could move. But I didn't move. With no one to talk to, to hear what I said. My mouth couldn't open. I just lay in the bed, my head turned, watching the door. I was worried they would wheel my baby in and then close the door and leave us alone together. And then what?

TIT INVADERS

IT WAS A SURPRISE that of all the things about having a baby, breastfeeding felt the most unnatural. Once again, the word *alien* infiltrates the mind. It wasn't bad, just unfamiliar and sometimes annoying. I discovered not one single warm, glow-y feeling from anywhere deep in my being. This *meh* feeling about breastfeeding was not what I had read about online. I had scrolled through the helpful hints and tips from experts breaking down the technical challenges related to latching and upping your production. In the first-person new mom blogs, I read about how it can start off frustrating and painful, but the accounts universally ended on something warm and uplifting: a breakthrough that happens one day looking into your baby's face while he's feeding and you have an epiphany about motherhood, nay *humanity*. A fleeting but beauteous moment when everything seems to fall into place and be right with the world—which makes all the heartache experienced ultimately worthwhile.

I could see there was a positive findings publication bias of a sort going on in the mommy literature. I could see why people who had a horrible time just stop breastfeeding and then keep it to themselves. And why would women who just feel *meh* about it want to spend their time sharing that non-experience? To me, breastfeeding felt like an act of hygiene, the same as brushing your teeth, sweeping the kitchen floor, something you expect to do every day, but not something you much look forward to.

Maybe it's not unrelated to the fact that I have never experienced runner's high. I cite this as the reason I have never been a runner. Initially, I chalked it up to some kind of congenital deficiency, but the more I read about runner's high it is more likely that I never pushed myself hard enough to experience it. Some researchers say that the release of endorphins and endocannabinoids requires your body to experience some kind of pain or stress. This evolutionary development served the purpose of motivating ancient humans to continue running after what they are hunting, or to escape a predator. In my case, once my body begins to experience discomfort it simply tells my brain to stop, commanding it not to exert itself. What's the old saying? No pain, no endorphins. So, I ask myself, *is that a deficiency or an efficient survival technique passed on from my highly evolved ancestors?*

At different periods in my life, I have tried to keep a schedule for jogging or getting on a treadmill. Running is perfect for me and my lifestyle. It's an activity I can do by myself, that requires little hand-eye coordination, and with minimal equipment. Being without chronic injuries, there is little excuse for me not to do it. When I have incorporated running into my schedule, it goes for a few months, until something else seems more worthy of the time, or I forget how good it is for me. My perseverance to keep breastfeeding started in the same way. I accepted, if not embraced it. I set my phone to beep every three hours to remind me to breastfeed. I performed the task the way I did other baby-related hamster-wheel chores like doing laundry, washing bottles, changing diapers.

Part of the reason I never got enthused about the whole business of breastfeeding is because it was such a black box. I had no idea how my breasts worked, and in the beginning, I couldn't be sure what was going on with the transfer of milk from breast to baby. There were four input-outputs that were hard to figure out: how much milk my body was producing, how fast was it being sucked out, how full my baby's stomach was getting, and how much energy my baby was expending to get the milk out. I tried to work it all out, but the only things I knew was how long my baby fed and the relative floppiness of my breast before and after. I didn't know my milk-producing potential, the factors related to increasing the rate of production, and the size of my child's stomach. Three equations, more than three unknowns. It was impossible to solve.

Sure, if you have the kind of boobs that spray milk out like a fountain as soon as your baby starts rooting for your nipple, you don't know the exact answer to any of those unknowns either, but you can safely bet that your kid will get enough to eat. My boobs didn't work that way. When I attached a serious vacuum pump to my boob and put it on the maximum setting for twenty minutes, I produced less than a third of a cup of breastmilk. Was my kid as efficient as this industrial grade pump? I couldn't imagine how he could be satisfied even after forty-five minutes of focused sucking. And yet, he gained weight and seemed sated.

The women I encountered in my daily life were all women who had their babies more than thirty years prior. They dismissed my worries saying, "Your baby will just cry to let you know if it's hungry." But to me it felt like a no-win continuous guessing game. I tried listening thoughtfully to my child crying, I tried to hear the difference between wails for hunger, gas, sleepiness, boredom, and combinations of the four. It was my body and my baby. I felt like I should have some intimate understanding about both, but I didn't. I felt incompetent admitting to other people that I had no idea what was going on.

Listening for the cries of my young reminds me of the main animal show on tv when I was a kid: *Wild Kingdom*, sponsored by Mutual of Omaha. I can still sing the jingle from the end of each show, *Mu-tu-ulllll-of Ohhhm-ma-ha is people you can count on when the go-ing's tough*... Back then, I had no idea what Mutual of Omaha was. I knew Omaha was a place in Nebraska, but why were they making a show about lions and giraffes? So, I posited that Omaha, Nebraska, was named after another place, probably some principality in Africa which encompassed some savannah. Maybe the king of Old Omaha had some great homestay experience in the midwest at some point as a youth and sent out some of his people to film these animals in his backyard so he could share the treasured wildlife with the less fortunate children of America. Maybe the host Marlin Perkins was a little white boy whose family the king stayed with and was asked to be the host based on their shared love of animals.

Anyway, no matter how this show came to be, it was from this show I learned that mother animals could identify their children from a crowd of kids based on their cries. It was also from this show that I learned about how animals breastfed. Sometimes while I was breastfeeding, I would think about those animals, creatures to whom breastfeeding was completely natural, because, well, they were animals. I told myself, you can do this, humans are animals too.

People say the discomfort of women with breastfeeding these days stems from treating breastfeeding as an impolite, if not indecent, activity to perform in public, to the extent that younger women have never witnessed another woman in the act. It's true most of the images of breastfeeding I can recall have been pictures: in public health pamphlets or on these lactation tutorials they have on the internet. The most intimidating clips I watched were about "the benefits of hand expressing" in which topless women use their bare hands to wring milk out of their breasts. They squeezed their milk into rustic looking clay bowls as if they were squeezing sponges, those fluffy yellow ones that look like they were plucked from the sea, the ones you used in summer pottery class or can buy in hardware stores to mop up industrial-sized messes. They poured the milk from their hand-thrown pottery into scientific grade glass beakers, as if you needed modern measured proof of the huge quantities of liquid women like them have been able to produce through hand expression for millennia. I imagined, because they were mostly topless in the videos and very body positive, that the women making these videos might typically wear earth toned peasant blouses, in contrast to the women the videos were made for who I imagined might be clad in black ballistic-grade nylon duo-pump harness-style brassieres, desperate to know the secrets to breastfeeding.

I can think of only two instances when I can remember seeing someone I knew breastfeed their baby. I have seen my sister breastfeed her children. Now she was someone who really enjoyed it. I can still picture her lying on a bed, breastfeeding her child, and looking sleepily but lovingly at her baby. It was a Hallmark-card moment promising the great satisfaction breastfeeding should be. But really, the first time I saw a woman breastfeed her child, I was 26, working at the California Sexually Transmitted Disease Control Branch and I had a one-on-one meeting to discuss the nuances of gonorrhea surveillance with a senior colleague. She had already started breastfeeding when I walked in for the meeting. The unspoken etiquette I decided to follow was to sit down and start talking, acting like the baby wasn't there. The same way I might handle a meeting with a coworker with a large pimple on their face. Look at them straight-on, but never appear to see or look directly at the blemish, even if it seems to be staring back at you. Once my colleague whipped her breast back in her shirt and held her baby upright for post-prandial burping, it seemed appropriate to interrupt the discussion to remark on her adorable baby and ask to hold it.

Up until doing it myself, the only place I had witnessed women breastfeeding in public was at an outside open-air outpatient clinic at a district hospital in Rwanda. I was there to observe the operations of an HIV clinic. The women sat waiting in long lines to be evaluated for their readiness to start treatment for AIDS. It was 2003, antiretroviral treatment was still outrageously expensive and there were waiting lists to get the drugs. At that time, HIV positive people weren't clinically eligible for treatment until they had progressed to AIDS.

Your doctor can tell you, and the poster on the wall at your prenatal visit can promote it, and the New York Times article can lay it all out: Breastfeeding is a powerful thing; actually, it is the very best thing you can do for your child. But there's a very different level of getting the message when you watch babies being breastfed in a public clinic, flies on everyone's tired, thin faces, and you know all the women there are HIV positive, and it's possible that at that moment, along with other nutrients and antibodies, the virus is being transmitted to those babies. You know it and they know it, so why would they continue to breastfeed? Because Breast was truly Best. And someone strongly and very persuasively told them to take that risk.

But while I was breastfeeding, I sometimes thought about those ladies waiting in line at the clinic in 2003. I thought about how much more agonizing their equations and unknowns were. It had been clear for decades how important breastmilk was as a source of nutrition for babies in developing countries. Mortality for children under five is heavily linked to diarrheal disease due to lack of clean water. And from a purely nutritional standpoint, however modern or developed it seemed to use formula, most women knew that even if there was clean water, there was almost no likelihood that they could afford a consistent supply of quality formula to avoid malnutrition. What was very unknown was: how much virus was in their breastmilk; how much longer would they wait for treatment. How much worse to watch your child die of AIDS than from anything else. So, at first we all had to guess and then later with studies and statistics we could say louder and with more confidence that Breast *was* really Best.

Since then, WHO guidelines and the availability of resources for treatment have changed considerably. Now, any pregnant woman should be tested for HIV in her first trimester, and anyone who is known to be HIV positive should receive antiretroviral drugs throughout her pregnancy and also the rest of her life. All this greatly reduces the risk of transmission while breastfeeding.

Knowing how it was in some places, it seemed ungrateful, if not professionally hypocritical not to try my darndest to keep on breastfeeding my own kid. I would think about that a lot all the times I was ready to just stop: when, not even discharged from the hospital, I struggled to collect drops of colostrum into a test tube; when I hit six months of exclusive breastfeeding, meeting the recommendation of the American Academy of Pediatrics; and again, at nine months when I started my kid in daycare and had to pump enough to get him through a five-hour window without me. Each time I re-resolved to get to a year of breastfeeding. I would do it, I told myself, but I also had no compunction about not liking it.

After twenty years of being a childless, single adult, the fact that your baby depends on receiving liquid sustenance from your breasts on a frequent basis is a major lifestyle change that takes getting used to. Prior to this feeding business, my breasts participated in an entirely different set of activities. They were objects of form and style with only entertainment function. They were part of being single, enjoying life, having sex. Honestly, I sympathized with my breasts. It's a lot of pressure for these carefree secondary sex organs to suddenly have critical outputs to achieve, especially when they have had no prior training or experience. They leave their old life behind and the way things look, there's no going back.

A male friend once told me how surprised he was to hear that women couldn't figure out how to breastfeed. Didn't it come naturally to them? I wonder if he would have understood it better if I had asked him to imagine a situation in which he was told that his newborn baby would get all its nourishment through a process that entailed sucking on his testes for half an hour every three hours for the next six months, and if he were a really devoted father, he should ideally continue this for at least a year. So what if he might have only seen other men doing this in passing at different points in his life, now his baby was crying, so he had better figure out how to get his child to latch on. It should be a cinch, since it is a totally natural process. He shouldn't worry if his testes started off flaccid, because as soon as his milk production increased, they would swell to the size of tennis balls and become as hard as walnuts. Just relax through the exquisite pain of your child gumming your irritated, slightly inflamed balls, most people find the latching-on to be such a joyful experience, after a while. And always bring a couple of pairs of pants wherever you go, because you never know when you'll start to leak.

In those first nine months, breastfeeding turned into my primary occupation. But objectively, as a career move, it was the worst job ever. Breastfeeding was a rote activity, required little creativity, demanded long hours, and offered no opportunity for advancement or lateral movement. And on top of all that, it was stressful. This job offered me no vacation time either, mostly because my child, let's call him B, short for Behemoth, wouldn't take a bottle from anyone, neither refreshingly cold or fresh-pumped, still-warm breast milk, and certainly not formula. I was tethered to the breastfeeding chair and my day was divided into breastfeeding shifts.

When the shift began, I'd start the clock. The online experts and the lactation coaches tell you babies need to feed every three to four hours and you start the clock when they start eating, not when they stop. So, if sometimes it took B forty-five minutes to eat, that meant I only had two hours and fifteen minutes before he was supposed to eat again. It seemed unfair, but there was no union rep to complain to. Often B took his time, sometimes he would doze off in the middle, but I knew it wasn't real sleep, just a power nap, from which he would wake more energized and with new demands. Other times B's attention wandered to my face or the curtains behind the feeding couch. And then I'd be right there, one hand massaging milk down the ducts of the feeding boob, the other hand tickling his cheek encouraging him to stay focused and efficient.

When the dragon slaked his thirst, I'd hand him off to my mom or lay him in the crib and start the countdown clock:

three hours minus however long that feeding had taken. That whole time B nursed, I was planning how to parse the precious time remaining: Could I make a run for Target, going solo? Should I walk up the hill and get some exercise? Would I have the mental energy to get on the computer and do an income-earning activity? Then there was that category of self-care activities, such as hair-washing or taking a nap. As a chronic multi-tasker, I also considered the potential for combining activities—maybe I could run up the hill, take a fast shower—no hair-washing—squeeze in a trip to the drug store to get some toiletries and indulge in a bubble milk tea? Or maybe I should go running to the drugstore, suck down a caffeinated drink, then walk up the hill and give up the idea of taking a shower altogether. The likely options fluctuated wildly in my mind, while I assessed whether B looked like he was settling in for a longer feeding or would suddenly drop off to sleep.

My personal priorities were also in minute-to-minute flux. I would suddenly confront the seriousness of my body odor, or feel panicked about my lack of income. I could be convinced that a twenty-minute power nap could cure most evils, and then persuade myself that an ice-cold smoothie would have longer-term benefits. My mind loved to grab onto these minor logistics challenges and cost-benefit analyses, because it felt vaguely like the spur-of-the-moment strategizing I did as a professional working person, negotiating and trying to communicate with demanding bosses and unreasonable team leaders.

When I was growing up, the only video game we had at home was Space Invaders—a stand-alone device the size of a hard-cover novel that ran on two size-D batteries. My mother got it for us for Christmas one year in the early '80s.

It cost $15, and my mother later told me it was the most she had ever spent on a toy for us. It was a big splurge. My sister and I had to share it. But we played it for hours, for months. It was great. But that was it. I never really played any other video games, not on the computer, not with the TV, not on a phone, not anything.

But one night, in the middle of the night, in the middle of the middle-of-the-night feeding, I realized how much breastfeeding had become a kind of adult video game for me. On the face of it, the objective was to try to get as many calories as I could into B. He sucked away and, in my mind, I'm going, *pew pew pew pew*, the sound I imagined of milk shooting out of my boob. B was gulping the milk down and I was racking up the points. I felt so satisfied, like the way I used to shoot down those alien ships at the top of the screen before they could fly down and bomb me.

But that was just the basic premise. There were many levels to this game. The goal was not just to fill up B; filling him up was a means to get B to fall asleep. And when he went to sleep, I could finally go to sleep, too. *Pew pew pew pew.* I knew I was close to getting to the next level. I felt his body relaxing, his eyes started rolling back and his hand went limp behind his head in an act of surrender. Soon he would be completely asleep. And then, *waah waah waah waah*, a friggin' car alarm across the street went off! B's eyes flickered open again, so I squeezed my boob to release a booster squirt of breastmilk to help him refocus on feeding again. I stroked his head gently to keep him relaxed, to get him in the gentle steady rhythm of going at it. *Pew. Pew. Pew. Pew.*

There was also the part of the game where I realized my fire power was not infinite, the more I pew-pew-pew-pewed, the more the milk supply dwindled. It was like I could see my power levels draining in that top right corner of my field of vision as I used up my fire power. He was literally sucking the life from me, and I was desperate to fill up my energy reserve again. So, I began stashing bags of chocolate chips between the cushions of the nursing chair; sometimes I'd be urging B to keep eating while a stick of string cheese hung out the side of my mouth. If things were going well, B was so into his feeding, he was not even aware that his mommy was doing the equivalent of a mid-air refueling. I knew the food couldn't instantaneously turn into milk, but I felt stronger, more energized with each morsel I stuffed in my mouth. I felt myself regenerating, pulsing with new power. I imagined myself to be glowing, with bright yellow rays of energy engulfing me and my child.

I've read my share of Buddhist self-help books that discourage multitasking as a form of mindlessness. In my heart of hearts, I knew the Buddha would rather I be in the moment, immersing myself in a single, focused action at hand. When I brush my teeth. *Brush my teeth.* When I wash rice. *Wash rice.* When I breastfeed my baby. *Breastfeed my baby.* Don't also feed myself. This is the path of righteous living. But I ask you, is it multi-tasking if you have to do one thing in order to survive long enough to do the other? In this game, my avatar was not the emaciated Siddhartha, but the fierce Mahakala wearing the five-skull crown that could shoot down the invading negative afflictions and transform them into edible wisdom.

After I had gained some experience with Tit Invaders, I took more risks. I was like Pac-Man, knowing I could make it through the maze of pellets, but letting the ghosts chase me for longer as I went for the cherries. Yes, I was Pac-Man—but not Ms. Pac-Man, because she wore lipstick and hair accessories and high heels while she was running, and I had stopped combing my hair several months ago. I finessed keeping B only half asleep but still sucking, because I knew if I kept shooting him up with calories, it meant he would sleep longer. And that meant I could sleep longer, too.

There were so many different levels to this game, and once you start playing one game enough you start looking for others. In the beginning, the short-term goal was for everyone to get some more sleep. But eventually we went beyond the "Nursing to Nap," and "Pumping Enough to Have Breast Milk in a Cup at Daycare" games. We mastered those and then I set my sights on this really cool one my friend told me about called "Night Weaning." Another popular one I was eager to try was "Cry it Out"—I was almost ready to try that one out myself, too. Like any video game enthusiast, I did it every day, several hours a day. I talked about it obsessively with other players. I thought about it when I wasn't actually playing the game. How was I going to get to the next level? What special weapons or bonus points did I need to acquire? I was determined to put my name on the high-scorers board, my user name would be My-Baby-Sleeps-Through-the-Night-and-Sings-Sweet-Songs-to-Himself-in-His-Crib-in-the-Morning-Until-Mommy-Is-Done-Having-Coffee-and-Reading-the-Paper. That would be the ultimate. I couldn't wait. *Pew pew pew pew.*

Some days, B would finish feeding, but he had only eaten from one side, so I spent part of my coveted feeding break pumping milk out of the other boob. I pumped religiously and poured the milk from bottles into specially made ziplock bags. I gently pushed the excess air out before sealing them and stacked them lying on their sides so they would freeze into sheets the size of dollar bills. They lay neatly next to the ice cream and plastic bags of mystery meat labeled hastily in Chinese that my mother kept in her freezer.

I often thought to myself that it was a futile exercise to pump and store the breast milk so carefully, given that B kept refusing the bottle. But there were some good reasons to use that precious time for pumping. For one thing, the lactation consultant said to pump—it would stimulate the supply, keep it going—and six months into this endeavor, I still worried that the well of milk would dry out. It also felt better. There is no discomfort like walking up a hill or cruising around a mall drinking a frothy iced drink while having one breast, heavily lopsided and stone-hard, weeping dramatically until it's relieved of its burden.

But secretly, I saw it as an investment in my near future: the way migrant workers put up with crappy living conditions and stash the money away; the way people put loose change in a jar to save up for a vacation. I pumped because I still hoped that one day, I could bundle up all those many, many small bags of frozen breast milk, stacked up like one-dollar bills, and trade them in for maybe a six- to eight-hour window of freedom.

It was the same feeling I used to have before I had a baby. When I was really itching to go somewhere fun, because I had been working hard all year traveling to too many small countries with podunk international airports, trying to provide thoughtful but completely unappreciated technical advice to combative local counterparts, when what I really wanted to do was to go to Morocco and meet up with that cute Dutch guy, write my novel, and spend the rest of the time looking out over the Strait of Gibraltar. At that point you don't care that it takes double the frequent flier miles to go where you want to go, when you want to go. You cash them all in and you say to yourself, *that's what frequent flier miles are for.*

Passing

AT 8:30 IN THE MORNING, the doors of the shopping mall are open. The metal gates in front of stores are still bolted to the floor, but near the food court a fair number of people gather. They are wearing sneakers. Some are sitting at tables, while others form loose clusters. Many weave in and around those who are static. The place feels a bit like a tide pool with bleached out coral pockets, a hangout for different groups of colorful fish and miscellaneous sea creatures. The groupings are part of the same ecosystem, but each group has only mild awareness of those in other pockets. From my vantage point, I see mouths moving, the sound muted, as if I'm under the water. I make up what I think their conversation might be.

Several cliques of elderly men and women walk while "talking story," co-mingling with each other. They all wear t-shirts sporting logos of establishment volunteer organizations (the Foodbank, Meals on Wheels, Aloha United Way, The Lion's Club): their baggy workout shorts go down to their knees. This works with their fanny packs and tube socks, a few push strollers with small dogs behind zippered screens. The most vivacious ladies wear bright lipstick and flounced tennis skirt bottoms. The latter safely cover hips and thighs, nobody seems self-conscious about their baggy knees.

"Hey, George, looking good!"

"Long time no see, you Buggah," some guy calls out, as they pass other groups. The energy they project says, "Hey, I can still walk, so I'm gonna walk."

"Use it or lose it," one of the women in a tennis skirt said loudly for anyone to hear.

"You said it," another voice responds for the group. Chuckles follow. Maybe somebody told them getting old is like being a shark: to stay alive, you have to keep moving. What's nice about this group is that any new old person must be welcome. A group of the elderly can always use a few more vigorous walkers, to keep that average heart rate above 60.

Maybe they're mostly using it so they're not losing it, but what's caught my attention is most definitely a mating ritual: The gestures used to get each other's attention, the demonstrated fitness having completed two laps of the mall's interior, the agility by which they weave between tables. This older group has coupling on their mind. At this time in their lives, coupling doesn't involve making babies. It's partly for fun, but if they haven't read the studies, instinctively they know that being in a couple will lengthen their lives. At any rate, going through these rituals makes them feel alive.

The group is all smiles and struts, there is some hard core cross-clique flirting going on. A mall cop might log in their morning report, "just some old gals and guys having good, clean fun."

The other type of creature in this ecosystem is me: a reproductive-aged woman, wearing yoga pants and a pastel V-neck t-shirt. My species all push strollers; our strollers do not contain pets. The way these groups form is still a mystery to me. There's the kind with a paid leader and an explicit objective—a power walk session followed by modified lunges which use the stroller push bar to ensure they feel The Burn. The other kind of group seems to be related through this life stage. Maybe some meet up with friends who happen to have similar aged babies, they mostly talk about their babies, sometimes they talk about their other young children. Once in a while they vent about husbands. At this stage in life, this kind of conversation passes for talking about yourself, group membership being mostly defined by who you are caring for.

The only kiosk open at this hour is Starbucks and it does steady business. Most of my kind accessorize with a drink tucked in their stroller cup holder, because "Frappuccino" means, "You're worth it," in the love language of Self Care. It signals to people that you are a tired mom, grateful for a pick me up, but you are operating in the safe zone of well-being. Talking to you has a low risk of your falling to pieces and needing some type of intervention or offer to take care of your baby while you take a couple of hours to shower, nap and otherwise pull yourself together. At least that is what I hope my cold coffee beverage signals about me.

I'm trying to look the part of friendly group member. But at the moment I'm a fish without a school. Since I'm not exactly working, I don't want to pay to join a group. And I don't know other people with babies. I'm an independent consultant who mostly works overseas and just moved to Honolulu to have a kid. Could I be the only one taking these laps on my own? Although I feel shapeless, sometimes I feel I could take on a new form, a bit like a cephalopod, it's just that my mind is too gooey to figure out what group I am in, so for now I'm trying to blend in with the surroundings.

I made an effort to join a meet-up mom's group earlier in my mommy-hood. I looked it up online. They held mall socials where they met somewhere to get to know new members and after mutual agreement that you are going to join the group, they tell you about their real meetings. That made me nervous, but I thought I should try it. The new member "trial" was going to meet up at the ice cream place, the sit-down old-fashioned parlor in the mall near where I was living. The kind of place that sometimes kids have birthday parties at, the kind that purported to have good quality vanilla and a marble slab to mix in your favorite add-ins. I thought *Why not? The worst that can happen is that I eat ice cream.* So I arrived the day of the meet up, about five minutes early. I didn't bring my baby, because I was nervous enough meeting new people, I would be a mess if I had to worry about whether part of the trial was to see if I could keep my baby happy and in a good mood while having adult conversation. My plan was to casually case the joint. Do a walk by to gauge the situation before it got too crowded.

First, I walked by the ice cream place. It was empty. So I didn't stop; I acted like I was going to the drug store to buy baby wipes. Then I came back a little bit later, but still nobody was there. Maybe mom's groups are always a little late because it's hard to get out of the house with kids.

I decided I would get my ice cream and wait for the others to show up. I felt odd buying ice cream at 10:30 in the morning. But I sat at the table with the most seats in the middle of the ice cream parlor and ate my ice cream. Nobody showed up. I watched for moms approaching the ice cream store with strollers. But nobody made eye contact with me, nobody stopped for a cone. Was this whole charade a convoluted way to check out new members? Maybe the real members passed by the ice cream place to see who showed up, then rendezvoused at the sushi place in the food court to discuss whether the new members looked promising. Had I picked the right ice cream flavor? Rum raisin. Was that cool? Too '80s? Should I have gotten a waffle cone to demonstrate I was carefree and knew how to enjoy myself, or did sticking with a cup show common sense and restraint, something more relatable? I finished my ice cream and I was still alone. Nobody came to ask me to join the secret mom's society. I looked at the teenager at the counter but then decided not to ask about the mom's club. Maybe she was in on it too.

I walked back to my car and drove home. Then I looked up the meet-up schedule to decide if I was crazy. Foggy Brain strikes again, I had gotten the day wrong. The ice cream social was the next day! I asked myself if I should try again. What if I went the next day and had to buy and eat ice cream by myself at 10:30 in the morning, again? I couldn't bear to face that teenager behind the counter. It was a risk I wasn't sure I could take. This was even worse than online dating. I chickened out and decided to forget the whole thing.

So, these days, I get to the mall, look around, pretend to be waiting for a group. Then stand in line at the Starbucks to get my badge of "Everything's okay here." My brain feels like the caramel syrup dripping down the sides of the cup. Maybe this is enough, to be part of the "Everyone is welcome" zeitgeist of this Mall. I am here looking for unconditional camaraderie, with good parking, flat ground, and air conditioning. I don't have to explain who I am or what I'm doing to the other people here before the mall officially opens. My story probably is just like their story. They think. I think that's what they think. But whatever they think they know is good enough. I think.

I tell myself it is okay that a big part of why I am here is because my baby has been up since 5:30 am and I am well into the middle of my morning, trying to find something to do. I am desperate for him to take a nap. To kill some time, I walked a half mile down a large hill to get to the mall. With the sun already high, I am covered in sweat. My clothes stick to me unpleasantly. In the mall, the skin on my bare arms feels cold and develops goose bumps, but the blood in my cheeks still pulses hot. Sweat gathers on the ledge under my nose, it drips down my temples. I feel uncomfortable in this skin.

I often felt like a voyeur in these early months, watching other moms, trying to figure out what their lives were like, what they were thinking, how they were feeling about their whole situation. It felt as if being a mom and having a newborn were not my real life. As if I rented a baby and stroller to see what it felt like, just trying it out, but having no real intention of staying. I began to entertain a fantasy of being a stay-at-home mom with lots of kids and a husband who supported everyone comfortably on a single income. The kind of mom that loved having babies and wanted more and more kids. This was her thing; it was her joy. I imagined being that mom. But I didn't think I could pull it off. I'd never pass for one of those.

Then I told myself, this is temporary, soon I will have to start working again, and all this time spent in the mall is just a short-term problem of belonging. I only need to fit into this role and do what stay at home parents do for a few months. The exhausted lack of productivity made me nervous. I couldn't wait to return to some kind of grind: wake up by a specific time, get dressed, rush to drop off my kid at daycare. I missed that feeling of having more work than time. I longed for a day when structure was imposed by someone other than my baby. I wanted a day that intersected with the outside world. Not because that world was so great and I missed it, but at least I knew how to be in that world, I knew how to navigate it, where I was going, what I was doing.

I started seeing a therapist about three months into this new baby experience. I was feeling on edge. Very short. Always tired. Overwhelmed. My dad referred me to a therapist he played tennis with. He plays a regular doubles match of fellow therapists and counselors of various specialties. It's easy to get a referral if your father is in that group.

"You need to hang out with other moms," my therapist encouraged me around that time. My therapist suggested I look for support and a way to get out of the house, something positive to do besides stare at my baby. I needed mom friends. "But it's important to find moms who you can relate to, or it will make you feel even worse." That sounded right to me. Except how are you supposed to find people who are similar to the kind of mom you are, when you're still figuring out what kind of mom you are?

I wondered if my therapist figured out that I am a strong Myers-Brigg "INTJ" —Introverted, opinionated, judging, not always good at starting up conversation with people, according to a cheat-sheet website on the 16 personality types. We form just two percent of the population, and women of this personality type are especially rare, just 0.8% of the population—"it is often a challenge for them to find like-minded individuals." No wonder it wasn't easy finding the right moms' groups.

The section on parenting on the same website reads like a description of a classic Tiger Mom. "INTJs are rational, perfectionistic, often insensitive, and certainly not prone to overt displays of physical affection...INTJ parents don't just tell their children what to do, though—they prompt them, make them use their own minds so they arrive at the same conclusions."

Good luck, *mon fils*. I don't think I want to be friends with that kind of mom, even if that's the kind of mom I was going to end up being.

When I hadn't figured out what kind of mom I was going to be, at least one thing had already been decided: I was a single mom. I told myself to start being brave, get a little deeper into the conversation with other parents I began to meet, at music class, at the park. I felt wary about how much to reveal about my single mom situation up front. People make an assumption that your kid has a father in their life. I think people think it's less rude than assuming you don't have one. So eventually there would be a casual reference to the husband I don't have. "You guys really have a handful with that little one!" or "Look at how big his hands are! Your husband must be excited to have a ball player in the family!" Then I have to decide whether to do an explicit correction. Or just pretend not to notice.

What makes the correction feel awkward is because it calls someone out on applying an implicit hierarchy of desirable family types. That having a husband is better than having no husband. Or assuming your partner is a man, which is more "normal" than you being a lesbian and that your partner is a woman. It would be great to have a name tag for the park that says my name, how old my kid is, and then a brief summary of my household situation, if not just my preferred pronoun.

"Oh, is this your first? Do you think you'll be having another?" asks a woman I meet pushing her kid in the bucket swing. That's kind of a personal question for not having yet exchanged last names. But I take it as she's trying to be friendly and the question is a lot on her mind lately. She wants to poll her peers to see whether they can offer a new way of thinking about it.

"Well, I don't know." I say, because at this point, I honestly don't know. A second one was something I definitely think about, but in an abstract way. I still live day-to-day, it's hard to think about big picture ideas. "I guess we'll have to wait and see," I smile and shrug. I used the "we" construction. I meant me and my kid, but it didn't hurt if others thought I meant me and my partner. Ah, this destructive normalizing, we do it to ourselves.

Maybe she thought I was just being a bit coy because she keeps probing, "What does your husband think? Is he excited to have another?" I pause to take a better look at her. She seems maybe in her late twenties. *Are you sure you want to go there, Girl?* I think. But I decide I want to go there.

"Actually, I'm by myself." Her face freezes awkwardly in a half smile. I can see the "oh" of understanding flash across her face. I tried to bridge the awkwardness by expanding on the thought. "I guess that's why I have to wait and see." The last part was a bit unnecessary, a bit too loaded with possibility as to what could come gushing out of my mouth next.

I wanted to say, yes, I want another one, but I don't know how I'm going to swing it. I have these frozen embryos in San Francisco, but I have to get permission from my donor. Really, I haven't even figured out how to go back to work with the first one. Oh wait, how much should I go back and explain about the known donor situation...?

I have to hold it all in, I have to plug that hole of big interesting talk I want to share with someone I don't live with and am not related to nor have entered into a contractual agreement with. I don't know what to say instead, how to fill the pause. The time to make the conversation just casual and interesting slips away. She just smiles and doesn't say anything more. Her child gets tired of the swing and they made their way to another part of the playground.

Something about admitting to being a single mom is a conversation killer. Most of the time I get the, "Oh!" expression. Sometimes I get, "I'm sorry." And then the person rapidly changes the subject.

I think the discomfort with my single mom-ness stems from a hunch that my situation seems likely to be dicey. Being a single mom of a ten-year-old or a 5-year-old, okay, that happens. You and your husband grow apart, things get stressful, after a few years of trying to make it work you get a divorce. But when you're a single mom and your baby looks less than a year old, then some shit really must have happened. Did your baby daddy cheat on you while you were pregnant so you left him? Did your baby daddy die in a car accident? Did your baby daddy not want the baby in the first place so he left you? Do you even know who the baby daddy is? Or are you so horrible to get along with as a new mom that your husband couldn't take it and had to bail?

Earlier that week, the 80-year-old neighbor across the street where my parents live stopped me once to admire how big my baby had gotten. "Now, you make sure you go back to school, Dear," she told me before she went back to her weeding. She gave me a supportive look. Holy Cow! She thinks I'm a high school drop-out. I look like a girl who got knocked up and moved back into her parents' house—baby daddy nowhere in sight. I wear my two-day unwashed hair in a loose bun, my ratty t-shirt celebrates membership on the high school speech and debate team. I look that part, a drop out of some kind. A drop out of my own life.

Maybe the conversation stops because they want to respect your privacy and they think you want to keep all this bad juju private. But I thought maybe they don't want to know because they just don't want to get involved with someone who may be a troubled, unstable individual. It made me really want to tell them more about myself, about how I came to be a single mom.

When I see the panic in their eyes, the words formed by their wrinkled brow say, "Look away." Then I feel like saying, "Hey, we weren't all left by a man. We're not all down and out, struggling to get by, you know." But I stop myself.

Because I know I want to correct their stereotypes about single-mom-ness because I'm biased myself. I regularly consume the brand of bleeding-heart liberal condescension posing as sympathy. I read thoughtful *New York Times* articles about the working poor, or the problem of homelessness, or the lives of refugees. I will express my sympathy by sharing articles on social media and pledge my money to any number of charities on their behalf, but I will give you all the money I have so as not to feel empathy. There could be nothing more threatening to my ego than relating to a person who is routinely pitied. So I sit with it and let that discomfort lie like a layer of old sweat on my skin.

In the first few months of having my baby, my friend in California, also a new mom, recommended that I check out a mom's group started by one of her friends, "Single Mothers by Choice." At first, I thought, *Yes! This is totally my group.* But then after looking at the website and reading about it some more, it didn't feel right to me. The philosophy included on the About page says, "*We have made a serious and thoughtful decision to take on the responsibility of raising a child by ourselves, and we have chosen not to bring a child into a relationship that is not a satisfactory one.*"

That struck me as one of those descriptions of choice that's not really a choice. It's not like I was in a relationship with a mediocre partner and then broke it off and chose to have a baby on my own. I had a baby on my own because that was the only way to do it. Their philosophy also didn't explain why it mattered whether a person was a single mom by choice or not by choice. Why is the support needed different? Why is the information needed different? Why is the social group different? I could see the organization's function was partly to shelter women who want to have a baby on their own from the criticism and assumptions of the people around them. But to me, it just seemed like a formalized way to show disdain for single moms and single moms-to-be who may have not have initially chosen the path they are on. The notion seemed faux-progressive.

And besides that, the website needed updating. One stock photo they used shows a white lady drinking a hot beverage from an oversized mug while sitting on a white couch in a white room, talking to someone on a flip phone. Come on, people. Get some color into your lives, reach out to the new millennium.

And then at some point, I feel ill wearing the mantle of a single mom, precisely because people feel bad for single moms, give them a lot of kudos, if not respect, and want to help out. As one of many examples, one afternoon I thought I would get in a real workout with my stroller and I decided to walk the three miles to the post office to mail a package and buy some stamps. I had a blanket draped over the front of the stroller to shield my kid from the afternoon sun. I wore a big sun hat and had a bottle of water in the cup holder. On my way back to my parents' house I stopped to catch my breath before taking on the big hill and an older lady in a sedan pulled over on the road next to me. I thought she needed directions, but instead she said, "Honey, I saw you when you were walking down. It seems like you have a long way to go. Can I give you a ride home?" That was nice of her. She had natural sympathy for a woman with a small child and no car on a hot day. I wanted to say to her, "You have good instincts, Lady, I really do need help, but it just happens that getting home today isn't the problem."

I have a lot of advantages that many single moms don't have. I live in a home with two other adults, highly vested helpers, who are retired and in good health and on the premises at most times. My parents don't need me to pay rent, I have flexible work I can do from home that pays well enough to afford a part-time schedule. That kind of job is thanks to my fancy education, which was paid for me, leaving me debt free upon graduation. By those measures, I certainly can't take credit for "doing it on my own."

With all my advantages, I wonder why I don't feel better, thrive even. Why is it that in these first few months I feel like, mentally, I am just scraping by? When I ask my mom to watch the baby for a few hours in the morning, it isn't so I can take the bus to my fast-food job without getting fired for being late. It is so I can get a little break; fill my mind with nothing for a minute. These are the problems of upper middle class single moms.

In penance, I apply the fortitude of a longshoreman, and continue to load up the angst to fill the dead space in my head, as if it is full-time union work.

As I take a last cool lap around the mall, I think what a paradox this all was: having a baby and being rarely by myself, but having a single mom sign across my forehead underscoring how fundamentally I am considered alone. I make for the automatic sliding double doors to exit the mall, ready to chug up the hill home. As I step outside, the humidity gives me a full body check, new sweat springs forth from my face. I've already finished my Frappuccino. I tell myself this is all just a passing phase.

Once at the mall, I ran into someone I knew from a long way back. She stopped me and smiled at the baby, "Hey," she said, "How are you doing?"

"Oh, hey! I'm doing okay I guess; I feel like he's eating well now, the latching is going much better. And he's rolling, and pushing up now, I'm trying to give him more tummy time, I think he's..." I started answering her as if she'd asked about how well I did on a test.

Was I passing or am I failing? Was I doing a good job? Had I prepared to be a single mom in the right way? How well am I performing? My honest answer being I'm just getting by. I'm using a lot of my resources to keep my head above water. I'm open to constructive criticism, but I don't think I can do much better than this. Sometimes, I feel like this part of my life is going by in a speed boat and sometimes I'm watching it as it passes, and sometimes I reach out to grab hold of what I can but I am barely hanging on, parts of me trailing in the wake.

I was so ready for the people I interacted with to evaluate me, pass judgment. But she was just asking how I was feeling, the same way she might ask anyone else who wasn't walking around with a baby. She was treating me like I was the person she always knew, just being myself. Maybe I am a colorful fish, maybe I am an octopus, how would I know? Why would I care? I should just be swimming through the water, living my life, looking for food, not questioning how I got myself in this part of the pool, not worrying about drowning.

CONTAINMENT

IN THOSE FIRST FEW MONTHS with my baby, the phrase "It only takes a split second..." kept looping in my mind. It felt like the responsible thing to do to stay in direct contact with my baby at all times, but that being nearly impossible, I allowed myself to travel across a room to retrieve things, if I could maintain eye contact with my kid. I was looking for tell-tale signs, in a blink, or a shift in focus that might give away his intention to make a break for it. Though at three months, the most effective lateral movement he could do was to shimmy in place. If we lived underwater or were snakes in a sandpit my concern about sudden escape might be more warranted.

I remember being so affected by watching the movie *The Diving Bell and the Butterfly* about how the author/narrator survives a massive stroke and is locked in his body without a way to communicate but then his speech therapist, Henriette, realizes that he could communicate through blinking his left eye. Except he's not just doing one blink for yes and two blinks for no, No, he ends up spelling out this beautifully written book by having Henriette, recite the letters of the alphabet in the order that they are most commonly used in the French language, "E-A-S-T-I..."and then blinking to signal her which letter to write down.

Perhaps my baby too had complex, beautifully articulated wants that he was trying to communicate to me with his eyes, while his pupae style body remained useless. M-E L-I-B-E-R-E-R M-A-M-A-N.

Unless his eyes were closed or he was secured in a five-point harness, I lacked confidence that I could prevent some terrible accident or escape from happening. Even then, when most of the time B lay on the floor on his back on a mat. Once my mother's friends came over and they cooed over the baby, but they noticed that he was lying flat on the ground. One of them picked him up and said, "It must be boring to have that view all the time, let's sit you up so you can see what's around you.

I had thought by putting him on the floor looking up, it would be like lying down on a blanket in the park and having an infinite view of the sky and the trees, thinking that was the most beautiful view in the world. Actually, not so much when you're inside and can't move your neck. I just couldn't always make myself pick him up. I worried about cultivating in him the need to be held all the time, because I knew I didn't have the strength to do it, and I thought there was nobody else I could ask to take it on with me. I wanted him to learn to be happy on the floor with me close by, without having to bear all his weight, all the time.

Isn't it funny, I couldn't even figure out how to prop up my baby in a sitting position. But when visiting my sister in New Jersey, she just positioned B in the corner seam of the couch between the back and the arm, and there he sat as if he had been sitting upright like a Buddha all his life. It was a revelation. *Why, I thought, hadn't anyone told me to do that? Why hadn't I just figured that out myself?* I, a fairly crafty, tinkering kind of person, didn't realize I could just experiment with my baby.

My mommy-mind was in the phase of nascent artificial intelligence in which I could only replicate what I observed directly or been told to do, I had not yet learned to improvise.

I tried to think of interactive things to stimulate him and hold his attention. I would show him black and white flash cards of shapes that might be useful to recognize in the near future: star, apple, squirrel, jack-in-the-box, chrysanthemum, etc. I would narrate our surroundings, my physical actions, the schedule of the day. I read him books, lying next to him and pointing to the pictures to help him follow along.

I asked my dad, a child psychologist, if there was anything I should be doing differently, to improve his development. I said I was open to feedback. And my dad said, "You need to leave that kid alone. Jesus! Give him some space!"

I pulled into a driveway. A man was cleaning his truck in an open-air garage. "Hi," I said, "I'm here to buy the...fence... you know... the gate thing."

"Oh, you hea to buy da pen fo' contain yo' baby?"

Yes, exactly, *fo' contain my baby.* I had driven through a mountain pass, to the other side of the island, to a neighborhood I never frequented, to someone's house whom I never met, to purchase a containment unit for B. He was now eight months and mobile, resourceful and determined. I needed this set of plastic fencing 26 inches high that could contain a hexagonal shaped area of 19.5 square feet. Standing in the driveway, waiting for the man to return with my pen, made me realize that most of the baby things I bought were contraptions of containment. A crib, a pack and play, an exer-saucer, a bath sling, a high chair, a stroller, all manner of baby carriers. All with straps and latches that could hold my baby in a safe position and make me feel mentally free.

Later my funny, Italian, I'm-glad-I-live-in-the-EU-because-I-value-regulations-and-human-rights friend would see my post on Facebook of B doing something delightful while standing in the pen and comment, "this is an abuse, to cage your child." But for me, freedom felt like a zero-sum game. Either I was contained or B was.

The many other baby things I had also served as tools of containment: A rattle to distract him and keep him stationary; a finger puppet that absorbed the imprint of his two front teeth and soaked up the accessory spit; a plastic cup with a soft chewable spout that dampened the shrill vocalization of his extended delight.

My heart felt full of trickery. I was the ferryman from the Grimm's fairytale who takes people across the river, then says to one of the passengers, "Can you hold my oar for a moment while I scratch this itch?" And then as soon as the person accepts my oar, I leap to the shore and escape. That's how I felt sometimes tricking my child into sitting calmly in a bouncy chair that seemed to provide some novel sensation.

Just sit here for a minute. I'll walk over to this side of the room, where you can see me, but you can't reach me. Just for a minute. And then when you're not looking, I'll disappear just a little bit more. Just for a second. I'll be right back. I promise. I don't really have anywhere to go, but I experienced relief to be out of his sight for just a minute. *I'm right here,* said my disembodied voice from behind the refrigerator in the next room buying me a little more time before B would protest. *I can come back anytime.* But I'll just stay here for a minute, I said to myself. Because I can, I reassured myself. Nothing bad is going to happen. But if it does, I'll be right here to fix it.

"Just 30 seconds, I promise," I said out loud. *I'm just over here. Where nobody can see me, taking a breath.*

You know the lesson of the story about the ferryman always focuses on the person who got tricked, the person who has to row for eternity or until they can trick someone new into taking their oar. But really what happens to the person who escapes? Where does she go? Maybe she has no idea what's next? Because she didn't think she would ever get someone to take her place. Maybe she's sitting on the bank of the river not knowing what to do with herself or what direction to go in. She might be staring at the person she gave the oar to still in the boat, who is just now realizing what had happened. And that person with the oar is staring back. But she isn't offering to take back the oar.

How awkward. This is a disaster. What a poorly conceived plan.

I can see how the idealized childhood is about being unfettered physically and mentally—the joy of running through fields of grass and tumbling down without cares as Laura did in the opening credits of *Little House on the Prairie*, the tv show. But can you imagine the look on her mother Caroline's face as she watched Laura tumble endlessly down the hill? Probably not joy.

Actually, Caroline would have been spared seeing it, because she didn't have time to supervise her children playing, she was hand-washing laundry for a family of six and baking bread and tending a garden, canning the fruits of her labor so her children didn't starve in the winter, sewing and mending garments so her family would not be naked or expose themselves, blackening her stove regularly. (I'm not sure why that was so necessary.) She had real occupations.

Whereas for me, containment was my main preoccupation. I had a recurring thought that someday B would become too much for me. Too big, too strong, too willful. A force that could not, would not, be contained. B for Behemoth. Really, he was a little thing, sweet and mentally straightforward, neither deceptive nor manipulative. But still I worried. That's partly because I'm the kind of person who likes to operate with a good margin of error. Not walk too close to the cliff's edge, not spend the full amount budgeted, I don't need everything worked out in detail if the margin of error is good. Raising B made me feel like I was cultivating nuclear power. Potentially I could do a lot of good, potentially, things could go very wrong, due to negligence or bad luck.

It had started with the breastmilk. B being a large baby and my milk supply coming in slowly, always there was the pressure to satisfy his hunger, literally. I remained uncertain that I would be able to do it, and if I could do it during one feeding, I had little faith in how long it could last.

What did I fear? That he would not get enough and that he would cry and be inconsolable. That's a feeling I think a lot about because of that book by Kazuo Ishiguro, *The Unconsoled*. I read it many years before B was born. But it stayed with me. The subtitle could be: *The Unbearable*.

It's a book that makes you feel you are in a dream-like state subject to weird dream-like logic. Specifically, you're having the dream that the protagonist can never quite get where they need to go, though it seems very important, and they have the intention and plan to get someplace. But they are continually thwarted at every attempt to make progress. And as the reader you can only observe, not intercede, though you are deeply conscious you are running out of time and pages to reach closure. The feeling of impotence is unrelenting. You finish the book, decidedly unsatisfied. It's a book that is uniquely successful in evoking the titular emotion. And now I feared it was going to become a part of my reality.

What if B became inconsolable and being inconsolable, he would not sleep, and because he would not sleep, I could not sleep. And with neither one of us ever sleeping again, we would, at some point, expire. That would prove what I suspected, that somehow, I had made this terrible mistake of bearing him without being able to give him what he needed, enough of what he wanted. That my fundamental mistake was not being enough. And that was in terms of breastmilk, but could easily become all the other things that he needed: food, shelter, stimulation, love.

I'm guessing that a fear many parents have is that they are inadequate and ill equipped and incompetent. And that single parents fear this more acutely because they don't have backup. And single parents by choice feel they bear the blame of being inadequate because they should have known better.

My sense of being barely adequate was borne out when B was about five months old. My parents went away for a long weekend. For the first time, I was going to be by myself in the house with B for three whole days. My mother had stocked the refrigerator. We had no reason to leave the house in the car. So, we did not. We stuck with our routine. I took him in the stroller in front of the house, back and forth, back and forth, walking backward with the stroller to avoid the sun getting in B's face, periodically patting the house key in my pocket to reassure myself I had not locked us out of the house.

In the house, when not feeding, B was sitting in a chair or lying on a blanket. My brain was in conservation mode. I watched television, but I didn't try to read the newspaper. I went online to check my email which rarely had new messages. I didn't answer the phone. I took a shower once while B was napping, I kept the door open in case he spontaneously learned to flip himself out of the crib. And would find him flopping on the floor like a misguided guppy. Or worse yet, with his footed onesie and his tadpole movements he might scoot along the laminate floor, and disappear under the bed.

(That actually happened once. I think. We were visiting a friend; B was six months old. He was sleeping on a low cot and I was sleeping in the same room on a sofa sleeper nearby.

In the middle of the night, I heard a thump, which could only be my inexperienced child rolling off the bed onto the floor. The room was dark and I crept over to pick him up. But he wasn't there. He wasn't on the cot, so I patted the ground next to the cot trying to feel him in the dark. But he had disappeared. I thought for a second that I was still asleep. I tried to replay what had happened in my mind. I remembered he hadn't cried out after the thump. Where was he?!? Had he fallen into a wormhole, been stolen by fairies? It had to be a dream. And then he started to cry. I could hear he was right next to me, but why couldn't I see him?

Then I realized that he had rolled halfway under the cot, but his head was so large, his forehead had wedged against the bottom of the cot and gotten stuck. He couldn't move, felt constrained and only then started to cry. I lifted up the light cot frame and pulled him out. Held him close and he went back to sleep. So I laid him back down on the cot and went back to sleep myself. The next morning, I wasn't sure it had really happened.)

We spent the three days like this. And for the last hour before my parents' expected return home, I lay on the floor with B in a stupor of boredom and exhaustion, staring at an eyelet bed skirt that offered an interesting pattern of circles and crosses in the negative spaces of the cutwork. B seemed sufficiently entertained. I counted the circles out loud for him as I listened for a car pulling into the driveway. Ready to pass my oar to the next person that talked to me.

As B got bigger and could do more than lie on the floor next to me, want more than milk or a nap, my capacity to handle things became more uncertain. My instinct was to contain the situation, draw the boundary. Partly for safety, but also to protect myself from being swallowed and consumed by this mommy thing.

I felt like somehow, I had to protect my mind. My concentration. My ability to maintain focus and get things done. I found that impossible in that first year plus of having B. Mostly because he was breastfeeding every three hours. So, he was always with me. Even when he was not with me. I had lost my ability to compartmentalize, to create a B-free space in my mental life. And that was disorienting. It seems ironic that for the gestational period your body serves as the boundary between your baby and the world. Then when your baby emerges, you have to devise a reasonable boundary between yourself and your baby. I needed a physical boundary to mark our mental and emotional selves as separate.

I used to be good at work-life balance. When I was by myself and consulting, I could dedicate three weeks of my life to getting an assignment done if I needed to. Sometimes it meant creating a situation where I shut out everything else to get the job done. I might spend a week in a country and literally never step foot outside the hotel except to present the final work product to the Ministry and then go directly to the airport. I just could order room service, admire the city from a view from several stories high, shuttle between meeting rooms and my room. I could focus, conserve energy, maintain my stamina and get things done.

And then when it was done, I returned home, living on a remote island, going to yoga daily, working in the yard, maintaining whatever schedule I wanted. That was work, this was life. But when mommy became my job and primary work, the boundary escaped me. My self escaped me. My confidence in my ability had eroded, leaving a thin line on which to try to balance.

Let us now take a minute to talk about balls. B loves balls.

His first word was "Ball.'" As in, "I recognize that as a ball and I want it." My feelings about balls are more mixed, veering toward the side of, "I hate balls." For what is a ball but an object that by nature and design will lead my child to temptation, to explore dusty corners, full of wires. Balls want surfaces, ideally glass cabinets to bounce off of and make loud rhythmic noises against. Balls like to do unpredictable things; they provoke unpredictable responses.

When B was a year old, we lived in a house on a large hill. The kind of hill that tour operators bring tourists to photograph from the bottom looking up, because it features a steep road that goes straight up, a 13% grade, to the top. We lived in a small house in the crux of a hairpin turn that wound up that hill. In the afternoon, we used to sit in the yard, which was shaded by the house at that time of day. I would toss a ball to B, because this was what he desired and I was training him not to throw things indoors. Being outdoors was a good thing, an attempt to get beyond my instinct for containment.

Mostly, I tossed a ball at him which would bonk him softly, but it would delight him, so we did it again and again. He had developed favoritism for a certain ball, a soft plastic open work ball in bright colors that was easy to grab onto. And then one day, B got excited and he flung the ball toward me, it flew over my head, over the short wall bounding the yard and onto the road. The thing sat for a second, and then because of the semblance of slope it landed on, it began to slowly roll. At first it looked headed for the shallow gutter at the side of the road, but then it kept rolling, bouncing off the side of the gutter and back on the main part of the road. It moved like a slowly trickling stream downhill, playfully, leisurely. My mind moved as if in stop motion animation. It seemed to take a lot longer for my brain to register what I should do next. My assessment of what the ball was doing came to my consciousness in a stilted way. But I had a handful of seconds to decide what I would do.

Should I grab B, sling him on my hip, vault the wall, and run after the slowly rolling ball. Or would it be faster and a higher chance for success to leave my toddling baby in our unfenced yard and sprint for the ball? But then would my sudden sprint encourage B to run after me and into the street? Would I be fast enough to grab the ball and then turn back to grab B before he tumbled from the wall and into the road? It came down to whether it would be more reckless to get hit by a car rounding the curb while holding my baby, or to get hit by a car, and have my baby see my prone body lying in the street, run toward me crying and trip over the low wall and hit his head. Then there was a part of me that wanted to see if I could catch the ball, what would it feel like to run recklessly down the hill, and keep going.

While I was considering the possibilities, the ball continued to amble down the slope. I looked at my child who was gradually realizing this ball was not coming back. His realization came slowly, but also picked up anxiety as this thing got farther and faster away. As it rolled around the curve in the road, just before we lost sight of it, the ball hit a rock, bounced up and caught some air, like an imp kicking its heels to the side with glee.

In this zero-sum game of Ball or no Ball, I guessed that there was no outcome where B would not end up crying. So, I held onto my wailing child and we watched the damn thing roll out of sight. Was it a symbolic choice to cling to each other, no matter who was crying? To stick with Us, and the good and bad of where we were at this moment, rather than chase a bright and shiny It, that promised something more fun around the bend?

I don't know. I only have the certainty of knowing that I hate balls.

THE FATHER THE SON

ON SATURDAY MORNINGS when I was little my mother would turn on classical music from the public radio station and then proceed to take out all the jewelry from the small boxes on her bureau, lay them out on her bed and try things on. This was considered a weekend activity at my house, the way some families go out for donuts every Saturday morning. When I was growing up, "extracurricular activities" on the weekend were not really a thing, at least in my family. On Saturday mornings, my dad would go to work seeing clients in a private practice, and my mother would clean house and do the laundry. My sister and I were expected to entertain ourselves after we did our respective Saturday morning chores, e.g. put away the dishes, clean the toilet, fold the laundry. And then we were left to read books or play with each other.

My mother had a collection of small jewelry boxes, carved or inlaid, or Indian patterned papier-mâche'd, carved of stone, cloisonné. I used to watch her take specific rings, pins, bracelets, necklaces and earrings from their assigned boxes and wrappings, and learn what went in where. Pearls wrapped in facial tissue; jade bangles wrapped in stiff waxy paper tied in place with red threads.

There were a series of bangles including one she called gum-gna. It was black and somewhat irregularly shaped and sized for a baby. Some of its cracks were covered in gold. It was a special kind of wood, but partly because it was so dark and it was kept in a box where she also stored our fallen-out baby teeth, I thought of it as a kind of witch's bangle. Something a wizened great aunt had given to my sister at birth probably infused with secret ill fortune. I didn't like to touch it. It was too small to put on, I didn't know why my mother kept it. She said she was saving it to make into some kind of pendant. I imagined her design would include the misshapen baby's teeth too. From a distance, they might look like freshwater pearls, and when a person came in for a better look at this unusual piece they would be horrified. I could believe my mother might use it as a voodoo talisman that she could pull out if we misbehaved.

There were definitely some gross things in her collection. She kept my grandfather's gold fillings in one of her fancy boxes. They were removed from him after he died. You can't throw out gold, she explained. My mother hadn't done anything with them. I think she was biding her time saving those fillings for the day she would have enough nerve to take them to her jeweler and ask them to make something out of it.

I say "her jeweler" because my mother always "had a jeweler" the way other people have a plumber or electrician. It was an important job, requiring a special relationship. It takes a level of tact to suggest how the good bits of an old piece can be refashioned into something more wearable. And still more to appraise jewelry someone has inherited and declare it to be fake. But no matter the special relationship she maintained; my mother never had the kind of jeweler she could take the fillings to.

One thing my mother had that I liked was a pretty, delicate gold chain with fourteen faceted red garnets in a wooden box. That was a necklace my dad had given her when my sister was born. When I was born, my mother received a blue-green opal with hints of orange fire. It was the size and sheen of a lizard egg mounted with four prongs over a simple round edge 10k-yellow band.

(I happen to be intimately familiar with what is the size of a lizard egg. Once when I was a child, lying on the living room floor, daydreaming on a Saturday morning, I turned over on my belly and came face to face with a small white piece of candy nestled in the carpet. It lay quietly, just in the shadow of the sofa leg. It looked like a Jordan almond, and without thinking, I popped it into my mouth. I was maybe six or seven, small enough not to think twice about eating candy found on the floor. It must have been the spring, when my mother on a whim, might buy a small cellophane bag full of pastel-colored almonds, because it looked fancy but did not cost a lot. At that time, in Hawai'i, Jordan almonds were the kind of thing you could buy in a nice department store, only at Easter. This was not the kind of candy you buy for kids. It was the kind of candy you put in a dish on a coffee table as a decoration. But if a piece fell on the floor, who was going to stop a child from claiming it. I had studied Jordan almonds in the dish on the coffee table enough that if I had put more than a second of thought into it, I would have said to myself "that is too small to be a Jordan almond." And in fact, it was not a Jordan almond at all, but a small egg, recently(?) laid by a lizard. I'm afraid even now to recall what the inside of a lizard egg felt like on my tongue, much less what it tasted like. I only know it was vile and I spit it out in horror, but I was too embarrassed to confess what I had done to my mother. I spent the rest of the morning thinking I might die and my mother would never know why. Since then, when I spy something of a similar size and color, I think to myself, "watch out, it could be a lizard egg."

These pieces of jewelry my father gave my mother when she was still in the hospital recovering from our births, were commemorative, romantic, and always felt slightly feudal to me, as if we were worth the value of the gems. Or would be some day. That he was paying her for delivering goods he had ordered. You could also look at it as some type of commitment—a contract sealed in jewels which she could display. She agreed to play her part in the realm of raising children and he would play his part to pay for things.

When I had my baby, I was hoping someone would turn up and give me some jewels to signal I had done a good job. Or better yet, to say, "Leave it to me, I'll take care of the money part moving forward." Maybe jewels are what you get only when you have daughters. Maybe when you bear sons you get something more substantial like a parcel of land, a herd of cows. I left the hospital with no jewels, no animals, no nothing.

While I was working in Afghanistan, a district health officer had offered an unclear number of goats for me to become his second wife. This happened during a dinner of the mission team and the Ministry staff to celebrate the refunding of the major project grant. My team leader was acting as the negotiator on my behalf, though he spoke only broken Farsi. It was a kind of joke that we all played along with, but I got the sense that the district guy wouldn't be sad if I took him seriously. It was unclear who would end up getting the goats.

I talk a lot about the raw deal of being a single parent. But one thing that is a perk is that there is no conflict in making all the millions of decisions involved in figuring out how to raise your child. A single parent just makes it up as they go. No discussion. No weighing both sides. No negotiation. I did really appreciate that. I saw friends really struggle with it, especially good progressive friends who wanted to do the righteous thing and not impose gender stereotypes on their kids.

Traditional gender roles provide a lot of structure to parenting: you are a man, and fathers do this, you are a woman, and mothers do this. If there's one benefit to gender roles in the context of parenting, it's that it eliminates some of the challenging partner negotiation in figuring out how to be a family living together. It conserves energy when you don't have to decide who should do what. My parents ran our family in that way.

A single parent divides the household chores among the days of the week, rather than the members of the household. I noticed that just as I wished to be rewarded for child bearing with jewelry, the things I resented as a single parent doing household chores always came down to having to do the things that a traditional male partner might generally be expected to do: carry all the bags when traveling, kill the flying cockroaches, build flat-pack furniture, and try to mount a tv to a wall.

But after the first few months of single mom-ing, my chagrin about not having a male partner was less about the division of dirty work and more the question of "what did I know about raising a boy?" How do you teach someone to be a boy, if you've never been a boy? I felt the responsibility to not raise a jerk. I wanted to raise B as a respectful, kind, dependable human. But I knew the tricky part was doing so in a social cultural context in which he was recognized as a boy. It would be so much easier if B grew up with a dad: a respectful, kind, dependable man who could guide B through the process of growing up male.

If I thought harder about what I was afraid of doing wrong, it was not about teaching him to be a boy, to like certain things, or to act a specific way. It was more that maybe just by being raised by me, he wouldn't be exposed to all the things he might get if a full-grown male lived in our house. I am not a princess, girly person, but I did not do gender bending things. I like to read books, do crafts, bake muffins, put on puppet shows. B watched me do lots of those kinds of things with mild interest. I saw that B laughed more when doing different kinds of things with other people: being swung around, given a horsey ride, thrown a ball. So I took him to playgrounds where there were little league and flag football games nearby. When I heard the garbage truck come up the hill, I picked B up and ran outside so he could watch two shirtless guys ride the back of the truck, jump down and swing the cans up to shoulder height to empty them. The garbage guys would wave and the driver honked the horn for us. When they realized we were a reliable Saturday morning audience they started hamming it up, whooping like lion tamers at the circus as they rode down the hill in front of our house. It was a very dependable dose of manliness on display. I hypothesized that early exposure was critical to being able to pick up the skills, interests, and habits of men, the way you develop an ear for other languages. Would all this effort make it less of a struggle for B later in life to learn how to behave, because the sounds and the sensations were part of his vernacular?

Gender roles in my work space/place have been a bit tricky. In many countries, it doesn't make sense why a woman my age and Asian looking is not married with children. It's not clear why a single Asian woman would travel by herself or not live with her parents. A woman in many places in Africa or Asia without a family or children is somehow not quite an adult, I think. Remaining single suggests a level of incompetence, a mismanagement of resources, a deficiency. Once during a lunch break with colleagues I worked with in Burma, I was taken to an outdoor restaurant. The server brought water and place settings which included utensils, a menu, and a personal dish of relish. The relish was a piquant dish of finely sliced onions dressed in vinegar and some kind of chili. It made everything taste more lively. I doused everything I ate with it. I wanted to be able to ask for it at other restaurants, so I turned to the doctor on my left, a woman slightly younger than my mother, who I had been working with on and off for three years and asked, pointing to the relish dish "Dr. Win, this is delicious, what do you call this?"

She looked at me as if puzzled for a bit, and then had an epiphany. "Oh, Dr. Ginia," she said, "this is an onion, have you ever heard of it?" It made me sad that she thought I was an idiot. But in those kinds of exchanges, you realize how much of an alien people think you are.

Once my work colleagues in other countries got used to me and my foreign lifestyle, I think it was more comfortable for some to see me as genderless. One of my favorite books is Ursula Le Guinn's *The Left Hand of Darkness*, about a foreign emissary visiting a planet in which the people are sexual but genderless. Something about that book captured so well my own feeling of having a fundamental part of your identity be absent from the relationships you form in a foreign place. Having to be at once formal and professional, and establish credibility and trust, but knowing a fundamental aspect of yourself is disapproved of or unacceptable to those you are interacting with. The local rules about how women behave and how women are treated don't usually apply to me as a foreigner. I am only there to share my technical expertise in a specific area, I'm not being taken in as a whole person. I'm not there to stay, so I'm not expected to follow gender protocol. I am not expected to serve coffee, I am not expected to take notes, I can sit at the table instead of the chairs on the periphery. And my end of the deal, I don't flaunt the violation of norms, I just strive to be polite and dress conservatively.

Let me tell you about a gendered curiosity in Burma that I observed during my time as an alien. People are pleasant but polite, a bit formal. Always very careful what they say in English to foreigners because it is more than likely that someone is listening and taking note, and may report it to someone else. The way Burmese people speak English is a fast, soft staccato in the rhythm of Myanmar language. Most people, men and women, wear longyi. A longyi is a 2.5-meter-wide length of cloth. Its short ends are sewn together to make a tube of diameter $2.5/\pi$ meters. To wear a longyi you step into the middle, as if you are a clown wearing a barrel. The top edge is settled against your midriff and you pull the two ends so the cloth that make up the diameter of the tube is flat and tight against you in front and back. Then you bring the sides in front tightly wrapping the cloth around you. The ends are tied into a knot and tucked in. The cloth is cinched around you tightly to hold the knot securely in place. On a woman, it is familiar, it is a sarong. For Burmese men, longyi is the equivalent of trousers, appropriate for both casual wear and business attire, depending on the plaid and the quality of the cloth.

So, a man and a woman will not wear the same pattern of longyi, but both are essentially wearing skirts as everyday wear. So, it was always a bit surprising when a senior official I had been talking to suddenly opened up his longyi, like a great bird ready to take flight, and retied it in front of me.

The male habit of retying a longyi is kind of like how American men unconsciously jostle their testicles casually during the day. They don't really know they are doing it but they do it often. In Burma, people will stand up in a meeting or while they are giving a presentation and untie and retie their longyi, just like that. It's a nervous habit, kind of like picking your nose. Oddly, you have to be a man (or a woman well known not to give a damn), to retie your longyi out in the open. A mysterious gendered practice. I don't really get it. But then again, why can men around the world casually handle their genitals in public but a woman cannot? I should have asked Dr. Win about that too. She might have said, "Ohhhhh, Dr. Ginia, that is sexism. Have you ever heard of it?"

A man's relationship to his genitals was just one of the many things I might have to explain to B when he got older. I started thinking about the men in our lives in terms of what they could provide as far as manliness exposure. I wasn't looking for a male partner, but the desire felt very primal. I was a lioness with a cub, trying to gain the patronage of a new male so my cub would make it to adulthood. I began to catalog the different male friends I had for these characteristics of being "recognizably masculine." This turned into a list of all the things that I was not: Someone who played organized sports, who commuted to work on a bike, who had experience as a summer lifeguard, who knew how to use power tools, who was a firefighter or a police officer. Note to self: these are all things that could apply to women as well as to men, including women I knew, but for some reason I was specifically looking for men with these attributes. Even at a time when my child could barely lift his head off the ground, I had already lined up a number of men who could instill in him a love of the outdoors, survive in the wild, or encourage him to grow up to be a first responder.

Can I tell you how troubling it is to catch myself fantasizing about traditional gender roles in this way? In high school, I took a women studies class senior year, when it was offered for the first time at my school. I read *The Yellow Wallpaper* and worried I shared the fate of the upper middle-class women repressed by polite society. I was intrigued by the notion of primogeniture portrayed in *Herland*. As a freshperson in college, I promptly signed up for Women Studies 10 in college and I came home at Christmas, raging against my father and the Patriarchy he embodied. I was ready to take a stand against the ridiculous masculine preoccupation with "mastery." It was subjugating us all. And I was not having it.

(Railing against mastery was perhaps a bit of a misstep the first year of college, but it did help me reject the medical school route as I embraced the reality that I was never going to master organic chemistry.)

My umbrage was based on a theoretical understanding. Up until college, I couldn't say that I was really discriminated against for being female. I didn't compete with brothers growing up. My father is a Chinese-American psychologist who plays tennis and listens to opera. He is a heteronormative male, but not a particularly macho one. Neither is my mother super traditional. She wore half-slips and pantyhose and foundation to work, but she worked in a lab and went back to work when I was three months old. When we were little, she was the parent who fixed the flapper on the toilet and cleaned the stereo components with a teacup of rubbing alcohol and a bunch of Q-tips.

On first glance, the way my parents played out their roles seemed very traditionally gendered. My mother worked, but she also cooked all our meals, including making us a hot breakfast. She did all the household chores by herself. My father's domain was the yard. From middle school onward, my father worked late one night a week so they could afford to send us to private school. My mother made sure we were fed at the regular time, and then waited herself to eat with him, so he wouldn't have to eat alone. She worked hard, but she didn't talk about how hard she worked. I only ever heard her express concern that my father worked too hard. She wanted us to appreciate him and express our appreciation through doing well at school to make private school tuition seem worthwhile. She treated him as the provider, as if she didn't also work full time. When he lay on the sofa reading the paper after work, he routinely asked my mother to get him a glass of water. He didn't say please and she never got offended, or said it was a rude thing to do.

By some agreement, they both acted like he was the head of the household. I remember, my mother never signed our permission slips for field trips at school. She'd read the permission slips over and say, "Get Daddy to sign it." Somehow, she thought it was better. I didn't know why. Maybe because whoever signed the permission slip had to be the one in charge? The one responsible if your kid did something unauthorized on the field trip. The person they call if there is a medical emergency and decisions need to be made. The parent who is really the official parent. To this day, when I have to put down an emergency contact for myself or B, I always list my father, I never write down my mother's name.

Now that I think about it, the position of "less than" my mother took on for herself wasn't about sexism. More likely it came out of the uncertainty of being an immigrant to the US. My mother entered the US as a high school exchange student from Vietnam, and then returned two years later to attend college in the Midwest. And then, after she graduated, she became a citizen. Only recently has she stopped worrying that when she travels abroad some official will look at her US passport and decide it should be rescinded. I think in our family, my father occupied a position of privilege, not because he was a man, but because he was never anything but American. For the record, my mother likes it to be known that she became a citizen before she married my father. You will get in big trouble if you ever imply that she married him just to get a green card. Growing up, when people assumed otherwise, it hurt her pride. And still, maybe in the back of her mind, she thought it was safer for my father to assume primary responsibility for the children, just in case she was deemed not to be legitimate.

That's the thing about privilege. There's a lot of extra just-in-case thinking you don't have to do. That you can't even imagine what other people have to think about. If something happens, you think you will just handle it. You think you know how the world works; you can anticipate the traps and side-step them. More importantly, you think the traps are inadvertent, not that they are made specifically to catch you. That's because privilege comes with a safety net that allows you to take risks. You live your life differently because of it.

And I think managing your own privilege is the aspect of being a man I felt ill equipped to teach B about. How much of being a man is about living oblivious of your privilege? When my friends meet B for the first time, even strangers sometimes, they comment, "Oh, he looks so much like you." And I look at him and I see it too, I see that B is what I would look like if I were a white male. And it makes me think about all the ways my life would be different if I looked like a white male. I have to think really hard. I can't really imagine what it's like.

WASTING

GROWING UP, I WAS TAUGHT to be wary of waste, even to despise it. Eat all the food on your plate. Cut the four-ply napkins in half. Have confidence in leftovers. Sniff, and then eat, it will be fine. And that was just the waste to be avoided when sitting down to dinner. "That's Wasting," was a harsh reprimand I tried to avoid inciting from either parent. Wasting signaled neglect. A lack of discipline. A miscalculation of resources. An exertion of material without return.

For whatever cultural reason, while growing up, waste always referred to materials, not effort. Perhaps that is the Chinese perception, that effort is infinite. And like the girl spinning straw into gold all night long, if you just applied yourself diligently, good things would happen to you. Like marrying the king. Just be clever enough not to have your first-born child taken right after they have completed a whole year of breastfeeding! What a waste that would be.

I had been warned, if you have a hunger to make something of your life, Waste will surely eat your share of success if you are not vigilant.

Wasting your life, perhaps this goes without saying, was the ultimate form of wasting from my parents' perspective. As a young person going down the predicted path of college and grad school and self-supporting work, wasting my life was something that seemed inconceivable. They never issued such a warning explicitly. But if you forced them to articulate it, to describe what that would look like, basically it would come down to a life you live for yourself, by yourself.

Basically, a life where you didn't have kids. Because wasn't all the work you put in to amass resources, have means, accumulate assets, wasn't it really about the capacity to take care of your family?

Maybe that's why they ended up being so accepting of this baby-making scheme of mine. Because it transitioned my single, itinerant life into something they recognized as worthwhile. The same as when I had the idea of buying a house in Hilo five years earlier, a place where I had never lived and knew no one, because a house is an asset, a tether to having a more regular stable life. It was a start. And lo and behold, it eventually led to a baby and my moving back to Honolulu. All I needed really was a "real" job and the threat of a wasted life would be comfortably defeated, a remnant of the past.

So maybe they experienced some secret relief with the birth of B. But I was feeling unsettled, like I was unintentionally moving toward something unfamiliar, being moved by an unidentified force that I didn't have a way to resist. The dread I experienced had a vague shape.

And then I smelled something unpleasant—something close by was wasting. I looked around suspiciously to find the source, and then realized with chagrin, the thing that was wasting, it was me.

My mind felt bound by a filmy layer holding its accumulated parts together in a loose sac. I knew I had forgotten something—something important, on the order of car registration or paying estimated taxes, but I couldn't focus well enough to think what it was.

The notion flickered across the tip of my tongue. And then...I had it. My appetite. It had been missing for almost a year. Before getting pregnant, I don't remember ever having it go missing. It wasn't constant hunger, just perpetual interest in what was at hand to eat.

I could eat when I was down, when I was excited, when I was sick. I, by nature a forager, was always on the look-out for something tasty. I sought out salty, crunchy bits, sour, juicy morsels, a secret kiss of chili. I could eat on a train or a boat, or while walking through a crowd. I could stagger toward a fish market at six in the morning and eat a bowl of sashimi without an ounce of quease. I could eat from a box, a bag, my own hand, even a leaf—in whatever way the edible presented itself.

I've always found there is something very satisfying about eating a meal from the wide, smooth surface of a banana leaf. It means that your eating utensils are the three middle fingers of your right hand, aided by the steadying presence of your thumb. This is not primitive eating; it is a practice perfected over a thousand years. To eat elegantly, you must know how to shape a bite-sized bit of rice into a ball with only the tips of your fingers. There must be enough dahl or curry or curd to stick the rice together and be tasty, but not too much as to get drippy. The hand must be precise to get the morsel to your mouth intact and quick to allow you to finish the mound of rice before you, so that at least two more patrons can take your place before the lunch hour is concluded. This is not a burden, because it is delicious. Soon the slow burn of chili reaches a crescendo. The fan above you whirrs furiously, threatening to decapitate the man passing behind you bearing dahl in a bucket. Sweat continues to drip down the side of your face. You attend to the urgency to eat more rice to salve your tongue. You are being in the present moment. You raise one finger and raise an eyebrow at the server to come by with another serving of green beans or brinjal. Then you scan the area for the man doling out gunpowder, a dry mix of ground chili, salt, and chickpeas combined with ghee and it is heaven, but it feels like hell in your mouth. Now drink some water before your head explodes. But don't forget to reach with your left hand, or the turmeric yogurt fingerprints of the uncouth foreigner will forever mark your now empty but still perspiring glass.

Eating provided my life with daily pleasure. At a young age, it afforded me a sense of accomplishment: At the age of seven, I was taken to a small French restaurant with its menu pasted in the pages of old issues of *Le Monde*, and allowed to order the rack of lamb special. I made my family proud by eating the rack clean, by myself, not wasting a morsel. I wore these accomplishments in my girth. By fifth grade, people distinguished between my sister and me by calling her the "tall, skinny one," and referring to me as the "dark chubby one."

My sister is built like a bird, something like an egret, tall, thin-limbed, and white. Next to her, I always felt like a dark, low to the ground mammal. When you're close in age, it's natural for people to distinguish you from your sibling by the most obvious physical characteristics. She's the one with the big nose, or the one that's cross-eyed. I often imagined us as Lucie and Mrs. Tiggy-Winkle in the Beatrix Potter book. Lucie is a cute blond girl who loses handkerchiefs and she goes to see Mrs. Tiggy-Winkle, a highly skilled washerwoman, dressed like Hattie McDaniel's Mammy in *Gone with the Wind*. In the course of the story, Mrs. T-W loses her clothes and Lucie realizes, oh, she is just a short, brown hedgehog! I always took comfort in thinking Lucie was not very bright, but at the end of the day, no matter how well she could iron, everyone could see that Mrs. Tiggy-Winkle was still a hedgehog.

As a consultant, the perks of travel included seeing new places and meeting new people, but more importantly, trying new things to eat and having people who could help me to find the most delicious examples, including those things that might only be found in their households. By extension, cooking is a source of pleasure that enables you to be around food—touch it, smell it, play with it, coax it into a transformed state. For me, cooking something I enjoyed eating was an act of self-satisfaction. I prepared what I wanted, how I preferred it, when it suited me.

After six months being a breast-to-mouth source of nourishment for another being, the most I did in the kitchen was to rearrange things in the freezer, so my pointlessly stored bags of breast milk could lie flat. And then when B started his foray into other foods, my initial adventures in preparing food consisted of blitzing a boiled vegetable with a boiled pasty starch. We were still living with my parents and my mother was doing the cooking for all of us. I wasn't cooking, for myself or otherwise, only apportioning and reheating,

When I lived in India, it was the same, not cooking for myself, not shopping for food, often just eating what I was served. I was traveling four or five days of the week; half my meals took place on airplanes. A South Indian breakfast on the way down to Chennai, a late-night chicken khadi on the plane back to Delhi. They were novel and tasty at first, but then became repetitive and then awful in the way cafeteria lunches at school start off being not so bad, but at some point, you can't dissociate the food from how it looks in the bucket of food waste near the place where you turn in your tray.

At my Delhi flat, I had a housekeeper named Hema. My parents visited me in India once and my father was charmed by Hema. "She's so pleasant," he remarked. Even ten years later, when he describes his visit to India to others, he pauses to remark on how pleasant he found her. And it was true. She had a lovely round face and a constant closed lip smile. To me, she was actually quite bland. I'd rather have day-to-day encounters with someone a bit more spicy. Someone who went around singing or talking to herself a bit. Who disapproved of the cleaning products I procured, or improvised a bit on what I asked her to cook. Someone who might expose the edges of her personality even to someone like me.

When I wasn't traveling, Hema made me dinner: a nice roti to consume with whatever curry concoction I asked her to make. Mind you, I didn't ask for specific dishes, I didn't really have the vocabulary for it. There was no creativity in my requests. I asked her to make eggplant, so she bought eggplant and charred the eggplant and made bharta. I asked her to make okra, and she bought okra and cooked okra with onions and mustard seed. I asked her to make dahl and she asked me, "What color, Madam?" And I would tell her red or green, or black. When I got back from work, it would be in a bowl covered by a plate with a napkin and a spoon on top, a covered glass of cold water in the refrigerator. I left my dishes in the sink and went to bed. And Hema would come the next morning just before I left for work and clean them before she mopped the floors and did my laundry.

That's what some call The Life. For two years, I didn't wash dishes, clean a bathroom, or sweep a floor. I made my own bed. I picked up my dry cleaning, but that was about it. And it was disconcerting. Not doing those things for myself made me feel like I was not quite a regular human. Not fully functioning, not using all parts of my brain or my body. Not living fully. Wasting.

"Why are you leaving?" people asked when I quit my job in India to move back to Hawai'i. There were a lot of reasons, but the most palatable answer I could give was, "I want to cook for myself again." I wanted to stroll down the aisles and put something surprising in my cart. I wanted to pay for vegetables without the three-act play of argument, scolding, and false flattery. I wanted to cook something exciting, and invite other people over to eat it. I wanted to be able to wash my vegetables only moderately well and not get typhoid.

(When my mother was growing up in Vietnam, she was not allowed to eat street food, for various reasons, mostly due to dubious hygiene. But, she longed to eat popsicles sold from an ice box on the street. So cold and in such pretty colors. She told me, one day she snuck out and spent her life's savings on popsicles. She ate so many, she got sick. Not typhoid, just indigestion. And for many years could not stomach the sight of them. She also told me once the most miserable time of her childhood was when she actually got typhoid. It's unclear how these two incidents are related except to say clean water and proper food preparation are worth talking about.)

At any rate, I made hay for one more foggy winter in Delhi and then moved to Hilo. There, I had five years of delight: spending two dollars for five papayas, making pizza on a cheap-o cookie sheet, and eating homemade olive oil granola and full fat yogurt anytime of the day I liked. The first few months, I sometimes forgot to pick up the cups from the living room and take them to the kitchen, because Hema used to do that for me. But this is what I call The Life.

The message I got from those around me, was, "Oh, but I disagree. That is called A Waste." Everywhere I went for work: Asia, Africa, the Middle East, or South America, my work colleagues always wondered, out loud, about how it could be, an unmarried woman and traveling all the time, alone. Even more so they wondered that I was single and yet I didn't live with my parents. For a lot of people in different parts of the world, those kinds of comments are not considered personal. That's part of your character, they're deciding whether you are a good person to work with, whether they will accept your advice about how to run their program. They want to know about your education, your experience, and whether you are someone they can trust. They pay you what seems like a lot of money, invest the time to take you through their program, and they depend on you to fulfill the contract with a quality product. Trust means that you will treat them with respect. Trust means that you will not throw them under the bus when the international funder wants to know why work is delayed. And when they trust you, they want to work with you again on the next project. So, you go back and soon it is several years that you have been working with the same people. And this is how I made the kind of work I did a Living.

But of course, to trust you, you need to let them in, and let them really start to get into your business.

"Ah, Dr. Ginia," they would say, "we have not met for a very long time. How are your parents?" They had never met my parents, but they always ask about my parents. "Mmmm," the sound of being very impressed, "you have gotten very fat." And very cheerfully, they puff out their cheeks and bug their eyes out to demonstrate how I appear to them. Pointing out that I had gained weight like that was something my mother would do. The first time my mother said it, it would feel like teasing, like a joke, but the second time she would mention it, she meant it was something I had better take care of.

I think some of my colleagues worried that getting fat was an indicator of something they suspected when they first came to learn that I was single and not living at home. Gaining weight confirmed that I was not preparing myself to get married and settle down and have a "normal" life. I took this mostly Asian-colleague commentary in the most jovial way I could. I slapped a smile on it, I giggled politely in acknowledgement, blew out my cheeks back at them to indicate there was still room to grow, and then I tried to move on to more professional topics. When they first met me, they had hope. They knew I wasn't young, because Asian people know how old other Asian people really are, but I was young enough for them to still have hope. But now, it was clear, I was crossing over to becoming one of those single, post-menopausal women consultants who have a Ph.D. and wander the earth aimlessly as a consultant. It's sort of like being a vampire. You look normal in the artificial light of over-air-conditioned conference rooms at the Ministry of Health, but at night you wear your true skin, and wander the public spaces of your 5-star hotels looking for sex partners among the host of white middle-aged business travelers and other development sector consultants. A fate worse than death, they thought to themselves.

Over time, it wore on me. I began to absorb the critique. Maybe I was too comfortable putting on more weight, getting older, not having a partner. Complacent in a half-way existence. Part of the declaration to Oscar on a balcony in Rangoon was pushed by a fear that this life was not a good use of resources, it was self-indulgent and that my potential was unfulfilled. That I was wasting.

It is ironic, then, after figuring out how to get pregnant and after delivering a healthy baby safely—making my "life-long dream" come true—that my body shrunk down to a weight I hadn't been since high school. People said I looked great. That I looked ten years younger. I fit clothes I couldn't wear before I'd even been pregnant. Wasn't this a time I should feel completely fulfilled? Wasn't this my Age of Aquarius? Somehow not. This was the time I felt crazy about the breastfeeding and figuring out how to inhabit the role of mom, a time when I was the least interested in my body and how others perceived it. I slept badly, my back was sore, and I woke up with headaches from grinding my teeth at night. I wore my new weight like a set of ill-fitting clothes.

And then my mother confirmed it. "You're wasting away," she said. Because I stayed mostly in the house, my mother had ample opportunity to examine me. "How much have you eaten? What do you weigh now? Have you been exercising?" It's funny, they were the same questions my mother had lobbed to me my whole adult life up through the last months of pregnancy, except instead of it being because I seemed too fat, now she thought I looked too thin. I was living under her roof and she took it upon herself to correct the deterioration of my physical body. In a determined, combative way, she started cooking pork-butt stews with taro, and rich beef broths with dates and goji berries. There were fat freshwater prawns leaching their juices onto buttered garlic rice noodles. I knew I was in a weakened state, so I ate dutifully and humbly. But I had no appetite. I had one eye on my child and the other eye on the clock, thinking about the next interval for feeding him.

It was a waste because my mother is an excellent cook. When we were little and she announced dinner was ready, you went to the table immediately and you sat down and you started eating. In the daily grind of things that annoyed my mother, cooking something and not having people eat it while it was hot was way up there. When she had dinner parties it would be the same. The last guest would arrive and she would start the last bit of cooking and then when it was ready she would call to everyone, "Let's eat!" Then there would be some dithering of people finishing their conversations and not knowing where they should sit. And it would take several minutes for people to assemble and try to figure out who would be where. People who did have the wherewithal to sit down as told, tried to be polite and wait until everybody took their place before they would start despite being commanded to "Just eat!" several times.

Meanwhile, my mother would be behind the guests with a large platter of something steaming to bring to the table as soon as they were seated. It would take forever for them to sit down and I could see it on her face, she was struggling to be polite and not yell at everyone, but she would be ready to dump the platter over someone's head if they did not just sit down already. You can tell my mom that dinner is delicious, but if you dallied around and hadn't come to the table right away, she would find your words hollow. How would you know? You hadn't eaten while the thing was actually hot. How could you appreciate her brilliance?

I used to think that was just one of my mom's idiosyncrasies, some weird aspect of her being a little uncertain about her standing outside the family and her cooking being the way to express the great volume of things she had to say. Sometimes it was boiling out of her. But until I had a child starting to eat solids, I hadn't understood. With breastfeeding, you are just trying to get the right volume of nutrition in your child. Quantity over taste and presentation. Their appreciation is shown in the form of falling asleep in a breastmilk stupor—your boob unattractively hanging out of their mouth. When they start eating solids, they start expressing interest in the food itself—tastes and textures, something that is within your power to alter. There is something super gratifying about your child's eyes of delight and satisfied "mmmm" of approval after eating something you've spent time making. From the beginning, B was a good eater because my mother was doing most of the cooking, and pretty quickly he began eating what we were eating for lunch and dinner. More accurately, we were eating what he could eat for lunch and dinner, but it was all good. My mom was very pleased to have someone appreciate her cooking completely unprompted or influenced by the rules of good manners.

Enjoyment in eating was one of the first ways B communicated appreciation for something I had done for him. He was a moderate giggler and had a growl like a feral cat when he disapproved of something. But this was at a stage before he was spontaneously hugging or cuddling. It was certainly before he was talking or pointing much, so it pleased me to receive verbal affirmation. Yes, it was enjoyment of a mashed sweet potato. So, his "mmmm" was more testament to the grower of the potato than to the person who wrapped it in foil, threw it in the oven and forgot it was in there until it was a sweet molten half-solid-half liquid mass. But still. I had bought the potato, I had put it on the menu for lunch, and technically, I had prepared it myself.

I started putting my energy into getting B fully transitioned to table foods. Not only because I was getting positive reinforcement to figure out things he liked to eat, but because getting on solids meant less breastfeeding and I was ready to get him weaned. There was a conflict of interest in this whole endeavor, but that is inherent to this whole adventure in parenting, so Bring on the Solids! I started making things, cooking more, thinking and reading about it to get inspiration. And it got some of my juices going. But cooking for your child is really not the same as cooking for yourself. I didn't add as much salt and sugar, I avoided chilies. I cooked things down until they were soft, I made things that could be cut up easily, stuff that would stick to an upside-down spoon.

I had started binge watching *Mind of a Chef* on Netflix streaming at night after B seemed down for the night. These were the days when TV was clandestine, at low volume so as not to risk waking up B in the next room. I would turn on the closed captions and lie on the floor half listening for sounds of B stirring. But then I got absorbed into the narrative of preparing cheap foods using high end techniques, saving heirloom vegetables and the reputation of backwater communities. I got hooked. I started cooking grits and making chicken stock, things I wanted to eat. I began feeling more like myself.

One night I planned to make a fish soup. B was eighteen months and rode in the large compartment of the shopping cart amongst the groceries. He discovered the boule I had bought in the shopping cart as we were rolling back to the car. And he began digging into the bag, tearing into it like one experienced with the way of a crusty loaf. Breaking through the crunchy outside to get to the chewy inside. "Mmmm," he said, appreciative, but not yet satisfied. He used his words, "Want More." "Please."

And so I tore another chunk off for B and one for myself as well, before starting the car, and then another piece each, one handed, as we drove up the big hill home. Munching happily. Later that night, we dipped more bread into my quick dinner, 20-minute fish soup Provençal. At first, we ate the bread like we did in the parking lot, room temperature and unadorned, at least I had cut off slices with a knife. By the time we were on our second bowls each, I decided it was worth the effort to toast the bread and get out the butter. There was good Persian saffron doing its job in the broth and the frozen orange roughy that had inspired the meal wasn't as tough as I feared. The bread, now crusty, rough on the tongue for a second, before the fishy tomato broth broke through the sponge, spread through our mouths on a wave capped with butter.

We were enjoying it. Each in our separate way. But also, together.

SPIT IT OUT

When we were little, my father and us kids always made fun of my mother's English, which is fluent but occasionally humorous and imperfect. She also talked to herself. Mostly in the shower, sometimes while cleaning the house.

In those years, she was coping with chronic workplace ineptitude, both from her bosses and her subordinates. Not to mention the people she dealt with in her own home. Often, my mother could be heard from different parts of the house, spitting out "Dickless!" as she replayed arguments she had at work in her head. "Total-ly Dickless," she would shake her head and then continue whacking the vacuum under the bed or down the hall. If her daughters did or said something unintelligent, she would look us in the eye and say, "You. Are being total-ly. Dickless."

She didn't mean we were not being manly enough. She was telling us we were fools, using a word but skirting its first syllable, because it started with "R," a consonant that thwarted her blunt Chinese tongue. You (ri)Dickless people.

It makes her sound more badass than she was.

No. No. I take that back. It exactly reflected the badass that she is.

My mother had a stroke last May. The CT scan suggested she's been having small strokes almost her whole life. It is hard to say when and how many. We can only see the faint tally marks on her brain shown on the scan, read by her neurologist. My father and I were surprised by my mother's corroboration of this. Her casual recollection that, yes, in fact, every once in a while, she didn't feel right. Throughout her life there had been moments of confusion, strange feelings she couldn't source. But they passed. The vaporous feelings in her brain. So she got back to her life, without having seen the point of mentioning it to anyone.

It partly disturbs me and partly comforts me that these micro strokes have been happening all along. On the one hand this history suggests they will keep happening, but on the other hand, it suggests they are likely to always be small, barely perceptible.

But this is a mistake: to hold history to its promises. These days, when we go shopping or out to eat, I walk next to her, always watching the tips of her shoes, to catch sight of a sudden dragging of the foot. My hand ready to grab her arm to break her fall. I think, what does it feel like when her brain takes a pause from the present tense and travels to limbo, while she has only the tinge of realization of its happening? Her brain observing itself being interrupted. And now that the doctor confirmed that it may be the emergence of a stroke, what different calculation does my mother make when deciding not to say anything. When is she sure? Does she wait to see how long the confusion lasts before it retreats? Ba bum Ba bum Ba bum. Does she wait several heartbeats, more than five, up to fifteen, before she will consider mentioning it?

Self-diagnosing a stroke is a flawed approach, I think to myself. How can her mind properly interrogate her brain? *Was it three be bums already, or have I already skipped three beats in between. Has it been five, fifteen? What was the count? Should I start again?*

With the stroke in May, her brain outwitted itself. She hadn't turned to my father and said, "I'm having a stroke, get me to the ER." She chose to be descriptive rather than directive, "My foot feels heavy," she said. So, my father took her to the hospital.

To act so immediately was remarkable for my father, a man whose own natural affect has led more than one person to suspect its delayed response to be a result of stroke. My father started driving to the hospital, not because my mother described classic symptoms, but because her speech was slurred as she tried to tell him about her foot.

The vestige of stroke makes my mother's tongue dry. These days she often shies away from talking in groups when the exchange is fast. It takes her too long to interject and stay relevant to what was spoken last. It annoys her to be waited on to speak, to be given a turn to share her thoughts, no longer able to parlay in the fray.

Yet no stroke or series of strokes keeps her back from forming an opinion. That mechanism is still intact, I can confidently report that to her neurologist. Her ability to judge remains uncompromised. Recently, I took her to try a bakery in a fancy shopping area. While we were there, the sunny owner buzzed about fixing displays and stopped to chat. She offered us samples. Insisted we try multiple flavors. I brought my mother because I knew they specialized in pineapple cakes; the kind Chinese people make. A small square of perfumed pastry encasing a soft pineapple middle, the ones you get from friends come back from China, Hong Kong, or Taiwan. The Chinese pineapple cake mimes the texture of a fig newton halfway between cake and cookie.

The owner was talking up her product. She was proud of it. No preservatives, local ingredients, Made in Hawai'i. She sampled every Chinese pineapple cake she could find. She spent ages trying to get the recipe right.

"And you've just opened?" I asked.

"Yes! This week." She gestured proudly at the new space.

Shelves of carefully boxed cakes. The kind of presentation derigueur for Asian tourist gift-giving.

"It's been a dream, two years in the making," she said, beaming. And then my mother interjected, she leaned forward like a turtle extending its neck to signal she was going to be part of the conversation. My mother has a soft, raspy voice these days. The stroke makes choking a hazard when drinking, so my mother forgoes water.

"It's not good," she said firmly, shaking her head.

She looked like she might put the uneaten portion of the sample back in the hand of the owner. A puzzled smile crossed the owner's face as if she noticed a bird had somehow entered her beautiful shop and stopped just overhead. She did not acknowledge hearing the comment. She cocked her head to one side and looked up at the ceiling, still smiling, but slightly squinting as if expecting something to drop from above and fall in her eye.

My mother's tongue had slowed, but it was deadly as it has ever been. That's not right, my mother would argue. Take it back. Her tongue has actually always been quite blunt. My mother cleared her throat and looked like she might repeat her comment to make sure she was heard.

"So what did you do?" my sister asked when I told her the story later.

"I shoved the rest of mom's cake in my mouth and told the owner, 'I'll take two boxes, please!'"

I remember, when I told my mother about my baby plan, it was still a plan. I hadn't really started trying. She often told me that after I went away to college, she and my father decided to stop telling me what they thought I should do. I did not seem to need their advice and I was so far away. How could anything she might tell me really matter. My parents were happy to get updates on my plans and experiences, but there was little feedback other than, "That's nice."

Telling my parents about my baby plan wasn't an FYI account of what I was planning or a fun recounting of a "that was a close one" after-the-fact experience. "That's nice," was not a sufficient response. I needed to lean on them heavily once the baby came. I might need to live in their house. This news affected them directly and the desired response involved them signing up enthusiastically to be part of the whole scheme.

My father reacted immediately, almost as quickly as he did to my mother's stroke. He was enthused. He looked like he had just won tickets to see Roger Federer play tennis. My mother went silent. Her lips compressed, my plan flat-lining across her mouth. After a while, I saw a twitch. And then her lips went flat again. No life. Just silence. Perhaps her brain was deciding whether to strike. Ba bum. Ba bum. Ba bum. At the time, we didn't know that she had been having micro strokes all her life. Otherwise, I would have taken that into account when I told her.

I half expected my mother would look at me over her glasses and tell me I was "Dickless." Yes, I would admit that being dickless was a large part of the problem. But she wouldn't have understood what I meant.

Finally, she said, "Why are you giving up so soon?"

"Giving up what?" I asked. Was she talking about my career? I was confused.

"Giving up on getting married! Giving up on yourself."

And then suddenly I understood what had just congealed in her brain. She had been experiencing confusion for the last 15 years, waiting silently for it to pass. She had been waiting for quite some time, expecting the pieces, my disparate, constantly mobile pieces, to fall into place. Ever since I became an independent consultant, my mother would occasionally ask, "When are you planning to get a 'real' job." Even if she did not make comments directly to me, she probably wondered out loud to people she knew, why couldn't I get someone, anyone, to marry me after all this time?

To her, success was built, like laying the bricks of a house you planned to live in forever: Finishing a degree at a good school, then getting a good job on the bottom, then getting married layered on top of that. Here's a pro-tip she might offer someone willing to ask: stagger the layers for greater strength. Work ethic, natural brilliance, decent looks—if you just put on some make-up once in a while—these overlapping attributes, were the mortar that could secure success to my person. Kids were the cornice piece affixed to this great, orderly structure of success—an advertisement to the fabulous address where I lived and to which my mother could point her friends to admire as they drove by.

That is what I got out of what she said. This was my thinking during her great pauses in between. When I announced, "I just want to start having kids, without having a husband," the whole plan in her mind was disrupted. It was the next link in an illogical chain of life planning she saw me constructing, it was the link that helped her reach her limit of silent confusion. A crazy way to have kids when having kids was irrevocable. No way! Some of her friends had divorced children that tried to online date, or went back to school to start new careers. But not once they had kids. You can't just give back the kids once you realize your mistake. It was time for my mother to speak her mind. Success looked to be in serious jeopardy. Having kids first wasn't simply mixing up the order of these things, it was evidence that I had become a failed state.

I felt sad when she accused me of giving up. It was my turn to pause. It exposed something I suspected a bit myself.

What if my mother was right? Had I really given up on myself? It did not feel like it day-to-day, but it was possible I was in denial. I could describe my plan in as sunny terms as I liked. Talk about a dream, years in the making. But my mother was not fooled by fancy packaging. My mother had looked at my situation and held it in her mouth a bit before swallowing. She was expecting a certain kind of texture and taste and this was not up to her standard. She might as well have leaned forward and said, "It is not good, this thing you have shaped your life to be." She might have spit it in a napkin and handed it back to me. She was not going to buy two boxes of this stuff and tell everybody how good it was. No. She was going to tell me to stop this foolishness before too much money and time had been wasted.

This was what I was thinking during the pause. Maybe it was five beats, maybe it was fifteen. It went to a dark place.

Until my mother blurted out, "What will I tell my friends?"

Ahhhh. There it was. The other side of the coin stamped Success. For a Chinese lady of my mother's generation: loss of face. *Diu lian.* When you learn this phrase, the illustrative usage is never described in terms of embarrassing yourself, the most memorable way to teach the use of this phrase is in terms of the collective shame brought onto your parents for actions you have committed. This is how we practiced using it the first time I learned it, in sophomore year, Mandarin 3. "Now class," the teacher said, "turn to your partner and have a conversation using the new vocabularies."

A: *Wo baba, mama diu lian, you shen mo ban fa?* My father and mother have lost face (implied: because of me!). What can be done to correct the situation?

B: *Zao gao! Zhen dao mei. Mei you zen mo ban fa.* Oh no! That is unfortunate. There is nothing that can fix it.

My baby plan had triggered my mother's worst, previously unimagined, fear—losing face among her friends. This was a more primitive but superficial fear. I tried to take it in this light. I told myself she didn't really object to my plan, she just wanted a way to talk about it with her friends that would not be embarrassing. I went with it. It took a while to talk her down. I chipped away with it over many months. The inevitability brought by a growing belly and a series of ultrasound pictures helped to get her on board.

Diu lian: to be clear, my parents never used that phrase when we were growing up. First of all, they spoke Cantonese. And second, they didn't expect to ever have to use it. The times they used phrases in Chinese with us were for those more *je ne sais quoi* situations. My father's favorite Cantonese phrase is, *som le…* which is muttered in response when someone, for example your spouse, says something questionable. It implies, "that person is crazy making entirely in their own head." He picked that one up from what my mother's father used to mutter about his own wife.

My mother's most commonly used Cantonese phrase is, *zhen a gaga?!* which poses the question, "is that real or fake." This is a phrase that evokes the idea of "the best defense is a good offense." My mother used it frequently to ensure that under no circumstance was she being cheated or tricked. It is effectively employed with people trying to sell you something, like a precious gem, in which case the next move is to physically probe the item and then to bite it to check for authenticity. My favorite Cantonese phrase growing up was *Bingo, oh-peh?!* which is good for car rides with your family and just kind of rolls off your tongue in a joyous way. It translates to, "Hey, who just farted?" That's the kind of functional Chinese that sticks in my brain.

My mother helped me a lot B's first year. My parents were both retired by then. But my mom was the one who was always there. She walked my baby in the stroller to get him to take a nap. She held him when I tried to get some sleep. She changed diapers. She cooked meals. She did a lot. But she did not say much. She described the current state as she observed it. She let me know when she heard the baby crying. She told me she thought the baby looked hungry. She said, today your baby looks really Chinese. Other days, she said, your baby does not look Chinese at all. She noticed when the cradle cap crap got worse. And then she looked at me up and down and said I did not look healthy.

I imagine when you have an involved partner, whom you like, and you have a new baby, there is a lot of exchange: "*Can you hold him for a minute?*" "*Did you see him do that?*" "*Can you get me this?*" "*Is that supposed to be happening?*" "*What do we do now?*" I imagine there are moments when you say to your partner, "*Hey, we are doing pretty good.*" Or, "*You are such a good mom/dad.*" Maybe sometimes your partner is inspired to say, "*You are an amazing mother.*"

When you are doing it by yourself, even when you are getting help all the time, when you are the one primarily responsible for keeping someone alive and healthy and happy, it is just you, talking to yourself about what is going on and what should be done. Yes, my mom was there, every day, through all the bits. But we were not talking to each other as if we were partners. I was the mommy, but she was still the grandma. I took the initiative, I made all the decisions, when to feed him, when to change him, when to try to get him to nap.

I was feeling stressed. My child was doubling in weight, pooping regularly, getting a decent amount of sleep, but I had no idea how it was going. I had words floating around my own brain in a jumbled, sleep-deprived conversation, but no external confirmation that this was going the way it was supposed to. I wasn't even sure the exchange going on in my brain formed a coherent conversation. I didn't trust myself to judge myself or to know what I was missing.

Yet, during those first few months, I was literally never alone. There were people all around me, one person in particular. And the whole time, she never spoke the words I wanted to hear. Was she thinking this is a big mess and it is not going to end well? Or was she thinking the opposite?

One day, B was upstairs napping and I was trying to get down some lunch. My mother sat at the table with me to make sure I was eating a lot. So, I started talking to my mom about how I planned to start taking on some work. Getting back to earning some money. And then I planned to move out and find somewhere to live on our own. I didn't want to get too comfortable living in my parents' house, having all these things being done for me. I thought I should get back to being self-sufficient and independent. If for no reason but to be able to say that I was self-sufficient and independent. My mother had some opinions about those options as I presented them. She thought it was a bad idea. She didn't think I was thinking about things right. It was going to be bad for the baby. And that made me feel stressed and anxious. And my voice had an edge. And in my mind, my mom was saying, "This is not good. You are doing this wrong." And I started to cry.

My mother was surprised. "Why are you so upset? I'm just telling you what I think. You don't have to listen to me."

"You're always so critical."

"What are you talking about? I never tell you what I think.

You just do what you want to do. I never say anything."

"But when you do, everything you tell me is about what I am doing wrong. What is not right."

"Well, if I see something that looks wrong, shouldn't I say something?"

"But you are always so negative."

"No, I am not. I don't know what you're talking about."

"You are. You never tell me when something is good, or I did something right. Always that I'm making a mistake."

She sighed. "Why do you need me to tell you if something is good? If it's good, there's no problem. You don't need someone else to tell you. You can see it for yourself."

"Mom..." I started, then stopped. She had a point. I knew what she was saying. You speak out when someone is about to bang into a pole or crash into a car they don't see. You don't tell someone, "Hey, great job, you didn't trip over yourself trying to get out the door." You expect them to be fine and know what they are doing. To be able to carry out the routine tasks of living. Things like breathing, eating, getting sleep. Indeed, my track record indicated my capacity to handle even higher order tasks: host a dinner party, make a living, set up a wireless router. My mother just added, "keep your baby alive" to the set of life skills she expected me to handle.

If you think that way, telling someone they are doing a good job because their baby looks healthy and generally happy is an insult. Yet, even today, I still find it amazing that my mother expected I would know what to do with this new life form.

Her thinking came from a good place. But I needed something different.

"Mom," I said. "I know it seems silly. But I just need you to say I'm doing a good job. Once in a while. Not all the time. But I need to hear it. Okay?"

"Okay."

I waited. Ba Bum. Ba Bum. Ba Bum. "Mom, can you say it?"

"I said. Okay."

"No. I mean now. Can you actually say it, 'You are doing a good job.'"

"You're being totally—."

"Mommmm."

"Okay. You're a good mom. Okaaaay?"

"Okay, thanks." Smile.

"Okay." Smile. Frown. "Hey, I hear your baby crying. You better go get him—"

"Okay. Okay. I'm going. Okay."

If I Were You

By the time I took my first work trip after B was born, he was nearly a year old. I had already planned to move out of my parents' house. It was part of the transition to "normal" life; B being in full-time daycare, working more regular hours, traveling again, keeping my own house.

There were a lot of decisions about the right time to move out, the order in which to take things on. Should I phase-in slowly, or do it all at once? I had ideas about it that seemed obvious and sensible to me, but always I questioned whether they were the right things for B. I couldn't get into his brain—it was still being formed—or try to walk in his shoes—up to that point he didn't even wear his own shoes. So I just had to use my own judgment for the both of us.

Just after B turned a year old, we moved out of my parents' house. I was ready to start working full time, I found a family day care near our new one-bedroom cottage. The first night, B and I spent in our new place, I cut my finger chopping vegetables with a paring knife and it began to bleed. It soaked through the paper towel I wrapped around my finger, and I began to think what I would do if it didn't stop bleeding. How much blood could I afford to lose before I should call someone for help? Who should I call to watch B? Someone close by or someone he knew well? Who would I call to take me to get stitches? Which would require less time to be away from B, going to urgent care or an emergency room? I even thought about whether we should go back to live with my parents until I recovered. It took five or ten seconds to work out all the possible scenarios in my mind and then I noticed the bleeding looked like it stopped. I went to the bathroom and put on some antibiotic cream and a Sesame Street bandage and went back to making dinner.

Mothering feels like a torrent of choices, calculations, and consequently, consequences. I think about the raft-load of choices my mother made about having children. My sister was only nine months old when my mother got pregnant with me. That alone seems a harrowing choice, like going over Niagara in a barrel. It strikes me in the gut how deeply her choices contrast to mine.

When I was seven or eight, my mother took my sister and me to the beach. That day, my father wasn't with us. He would have been working our plot at the community garden or at home listening to the Saturday afternoon Live at the Met broadcast or out somewhere playing tennis with a friend. The strip of sand my mother brought us to was called Sans Souci. It was bordered by a low rock wall. As my mother stepped over the wall, she tripped and cut her leg deeply. The gash was more than six inches long and bled a lot. My mother sat on the ground holding her shin together trying to stop the bleeding. Then she took the picnic blanket she was carrying, and draped it over her head and body. We could see her form under the blanket rocking back and forth. She looked like a boat trying to stay afloat in a rough sea. I think she was crying silently and didn't want us to see her face. She knew she had to get herself to an emergency room. She composed herself and came out from under the blanket. Then she did something unexpected, which I will never forget.

She had one hand on me and one hand on my sister and she looked us in the eyes and said, "Stay by this wall, I'm going to get my leg fixed, then I'm coming back here to find you." She paused, assessed comprehension. And then we watched her hobble away toward the car parked some distance away.

And so we sat there.

The reason my mother took us to the beach that day was not to play in the sand or frolic in the waves. We hardly went to the beach as kids, and never just with her, because my mother had never learned how to swim. Instead, she took us to the library twice a week. We played with the neighborhood kids on the common grass in front of our town house. Sometimes we tagged along to a silk flower making class my mother took. And we watched a ton of TV. Back then, our very favorite prime time show was called *Real People*, it was the type of reality show of its time in which a group of hosts introduced and then showed short, taped segments of regular people doing interesting, if not amazing things.

And the odd reason my mother took us to the beach that day was because the hosts of that show, that we loved so much, were taping in Hawai'i and using the ocean at San Souci beach as their backdrop. My sister and I were surprised that we were getting to go. And we were even more surprised to end up being left at the beach with instructions to sit tight in one spot for an uncertain period of time until my mother returned.

In the thirty seconds my mother took instructing us in how to handle our abandonment, she told us we could go to see *Real People* if we came back to that exact spot on the wall afterward. What was she thinking? Clearly, she had made some calculations. First, to decide to leave us and then to think that we would be bored just sitting there and then to estimate that we could be relied upon to go to the show and then come back as instructed. I imagine she was thinking things like: did she remember where she parked the car; was she going to get lost on the way to the emergency room, could she get everything done in time to get us home to make dinner. Those were the kinds of things I remember my mother being challenged by day to day.

Mothers make these calculations all the time. I know. My mother was a chemist. So I think of her as a scientist. To me, she seemed very confident in her judgment about us kids, though at times it confused me. Growing up, in the shower there was always a green bottle decorated with a pattern of hexagons, labeled Phisoderm. Always there, but hardly used. My mother referred to it as Phisohex. That made it sound more sinister to me, as was her warning: "Don't use it unless I tell you to," my mother said. And "If you touch the bottle, wash your hands really, really good." When we were a little older, she added, "or you'll get brain damaged." English wasn't her first language, but she had a way with words. I remember thinking, wash your hands really good, or you'll get brain damage?!?! Why did we keep this bottle of poison in the shower? And why every once in a while, did she instruct us to use it on our bodies! She did this when we got especially weird rashes or were afflicted with strange, stinky smells. She supervised us as we stayed in the shower extra-long to make sure everything got washed off. We were skeptical but did as she told us to do.

Later, I read online that in 1972 that product had been recalled because of having too high a concentration of hexachlorophene, which was associated with 54 cases of brain damage and death. I was born in 1974, so presumably they had changed the formula before my mother started using Phisohex on us. I'm sure my mother had made some thorough calculation about the effectiveness of the new formula vis-a-vis the alternatives and the likelihood that it had really passed the safety standards. It was the equivalent of decisions I make for my baby about non-BPA bottles, car seats, and co-sleeping. Some decisions are arbitrary, some decisions are made by instinct, others informed by data. Scientist or not? What to do? Who's to judge?

There are so many questions I want to ask my mother about the day she left us at the beach. I want to know why she didn't take us with her to the hospital. Did she think we would slow her down trying to get to the car? Was she afraid she would pass out while driving and kill us all? Did she just not want us to see her panic? Did she think we would be that disappointed about not seeing *Real People*?

From where my sister and I were sitting on the rock wall, we could see the stage they had erected on the beach for *Real People*. We could see the crowds beginning to form around a taped off area where the hosts were going to perform. We definitely could have walked the 100 yards straight ahead and seen what we came to see, and returned. But we didn't. We stayed on the wall and scanned left and right for my mother, with her fixed leg, to come back. I don't remember any conversation with my sister. We were not chatting about stupid things. We were not giving each other false comfort or encouragement. We were sober and silent, focused on scouring the horizon with our eyes.

Recently, I asked my sister what she remembers about that day, and unbelievable to me, she says she hardly remembers this incident. Even though she is older and presumably the one in charge of us that day. At that age, I was noticeably bossier and even today people think I may be the older one. But even if she didn't think she was in charge, how can she not remember? What would we have done if our mother had not come back?

It's easy to judge this situation and to say I would never do that. How could she just leave her kids like that? I can say I wouldn't have made the same decision if that happened to me, but it's because I know I wouldn't have to.

My parenting resources are so different today than my mother's were at the time. In the 1980s, nobody had cell phones. Even with a pay phone, my mother realized she couldn't have reached my father for help, because he probably was not in the house near a phone. Even if she reached him, they only had one car at the time, so it would have taken him a while to find a friend to give him a ride to come get us or take her to the hospital. It is not easy to flag a taxi at the beach, and there was no ride-share service she could have called. We didn't have much money then and she would have thought hard about spending the money to get a taxi to get us to the hospital or even as far as the car. The only family we had in Hawai'i was my father's side and I think my mother had a different relationship with her in-laws at the time. She never would have called them. And for many reasons, including that she came to the United States as an exchange student, it would never occur to my mother to expose her vulnerability to a stranger on the beach and ask them to help.

I think about what I would do. If I didn't have my phone with me, I would most definitely ask a stranger to borrow theirs. I would call my parents to pick me up, or if I didn't think I had enough blood left in my body, I would ask someone to call 9-1-1 and feel confident my health insurance would cover it. And before I passed out, I would write down the names and phone numbers of people who could be called to tell them what happened and to come get my kids. I would uncover my leg and let the people around me know I needed some serious help.

It seems impossible to consider leaving my kids by themselves at the beach with an indefinite plan, no temporary guardian. But if I left my kids to sit in a public place, I would haul out my raggedy mom bag and fish in its depths for a hat and sunscreen. I would leave them the bag and make sure they knew inside was an insulated water bottle and assorted single serving bag of pretzels or graham crackers or goldfish. That's not a comment on the kind of mother I am, it's the way norms have changed about how moms mind their kids. I would fold up a $20 bill and tuck it into their pocket before being on my way. It seems inconceivable that my mother didn't even leave us a quarter to be able to use a pay phone. I supposed she thought she was the only one we would think to call so then what would be the use?

In my memory, my sister and I sat on the wall all that afternoon. And eventually, my mother came back. I have no way to tell how long we really waited. She pulled up in the car, as if she was picking us up from school. We piled in as usual; we probably didn't use seat belts because at that time it was not the law to use them in the back. We probably drove home, and then she made dinner. She had large ugly, black stitches up and down the front of her lower leg for a while. To me, it looked like she had bought a sewing kit from a drug store and sat down to do it herself. My mother was always thin and it seemed hard to see how they had enough flesh for a needle to grab onto so the wound could close.

It's been more than 40 years and my mother still has that scar. I don't know if she notices it herself anymore. At the kitchen table, she often sits with one knee bent, foot on the seat while she works or reads, and I see it. Sometimes I look down at my own shins and notice that the odd pigmentation of skin getting older resembles that of my mother's. One day, I will point out the faint old gash and ask her to tell me the story of how she got it.

Epilogue: Sublimation

IT IS AFTER FINISHING B'S GOING-TO-BED ROUTINE when I really need a cold glass of ice water to decompress. But in my new place the ice trays are always empty. It's not that I don't fill them in the first place, but it takes me so long to empty them into the bin that they sublimate into vapor. I never empty them at night because the cracking noise is so loud that I don't want to wake B, and I never remember to do it in the day when I'm home alone and it doesn't matter. So, I never get that glass of really cold water.

When I was living at my parents' house it wasn't a problem. They have the kind of refrigerator a comfortable upper-middle class retired couple has, the kind that makes ice by itself. Not the kind that has an ice dispenser in the door, but still, the ice gets unleashed from its trays automatically and this makes for a lot more ice. It is convenient and comfortable and this issue of sublimation is almost unheard of.

It is easy to feel envious of another person's ice maker. I am easily distracted by envy. But the point of mentioning the ice was to talk about sublimation. Because sublimation perfectly captures my own change of state; the process of transforming from an incompetent, wild-with-anxiety-new-mom into a now-I'm-coasting-mom-of-a-toddler. I went from solid to gas, frozen to floating. The phase change happened partly because postpartum frazzle is not a stable state. Partly, I habituated to the unpredictability of B's wants, and simultaneously B, himself, just became easier to handle. It happened to me without purposeful, strategic effort. I hadn't observed my own transition, just one day recognized a more buoyant feeling in my body and my imagination.

Some days, I drop B off at daycare and continue down the road circling Diamond Head toward the beach. I take my computer and have a second working breakfast at a shady beachside café. The view is beautiful, the breeze soothing, and my mind bobs gently as if sometimes in the water and sometimes drifting in the wind. At adjacent picnic tables I often see young Japanese tourist couples with small babies, barely able to sit up on their own, enjoying the view. These families are on vacation, so at the moment, they have all the time in the world. Their main activity seems to be smiling and sitting quietly with each other. Sometimes they share a smoothie or a cappuccino, but often they all sit side by side, facing outward, toward the water just taking in the day.

I sit facing the ocean too, pretending to be enjoying the view, but I am really pretending to be them, enjoying what must be their view. These are the moments I feel the most envious of coupled-parents that I ever do. This moment of just being together, not having to talk, but immersed in a completely mutual moment that they will remember for a long time. More than a photo of the great vacation they had in Hawai'i, they will remember the feeling of being together, easy, beautiful, blessed. It isn't that I don't have moments of peace with B, but these are by myself and the ability to share them with someone else you love as much as your child, and who has played a part in creating the moment as much as you, isn't there.

What I wouldn't give, I think to myself. The thought is reflexive. But I know that the other way is better. Now that I have sublimated, I can touch that thought and let it evaporate, know it remains in the atmosphere nearby. I don't really think twice about having done it the way I did. I wouldn't give much to change it. Because it is possible to feel things are perfect, and still know a way it could be better.

Afterward

This is a very personal story I have been working at off and on for ten years and in preparing for it to be published I am simultaneously freaked out that no one will read it and that someone will actually read it. Several people said I could always use a pen name to get around the latter discomfort, but that would surely arouse your suspicions. Why would you bother to read somebody's story if they couldn't even put their own name on it?

So I've embraced the soft, touchy, smelly parts and shared what is intended to be a "true" story. And yet I worry that the people who were there with me as it happened might not totally recognize me, much less themselves as they read it. Their memory of all this being different than how I tell it. So, does that disqualify this book from being a candid and honest telling?

Way back in graduate school, I took a seminar on qualitative methods for data analysis and we read Jeffrey Prager's *Presenting the Past*, in which he makes the case for memory being a construct of a person's experience and the emotional resonance of the experience both at the time of the event and at the time of remembering. And that memory is further influenced by a person's specific social context and the broader social norms and culture at both time points. Whew, I'm glad that was pulled out of the deepest recesses of my brain. Remembering I learned that helps me reconcile my intention to write something real, even if there is some dispute with my contemporaries about how it was.

To complicate the matter further, I now call upon teachings attributed to the other big "B" —i.e. the Buddha, who might remind us that while this *is* my story, *I* am not my story. Pause to absorb that. Whoever wrote that down and then repeated it to others meant that the notion that there is a Story which describes your True Self, falsely fixes you to a point in time and what you did and said and thought at that time. *This* notion of trying to remain the Self in this story is just attachment to Ego, and we all know that this kind of attachment is a well-tested recipe for Preventable Suffering.

Nobody wants that. No need to serve that up to guests, trussed up and perched on a beer can, or to make a special effort for that to be one of your child's first foods. No need, brah. Breathe easy. Let go. I say to myself.

And while I feel a bit more at ease in telling this story as I remember it, I do want to respect the privacy of those I describe who may not be interested in sharing their part in my story in such a public way. This is especially true for my donor. The decision not to describe him in much detail or speculate on his thought process or recount our conversations is an attempt to show this respect.

Many of the names of people who played a role in this story have been changed as well. I realize that my family, although unnamed, cannot help but be identified. But what can be done about that? They have thrown up their hands and said "What can we do but buy several copies and send them to our friends?" Please follow suit.

ACKNOWLEDGEMENTS

My deepest thanks go to Ruth and Don of Saddle Road Press, most recently for their encouragement, editing, and beautiful design work and, for many years, in creating a space to write and talk and think, over much pie and cake.

For working through many of the earliest written chapters and helping me to try this voice out, I am grateful for the Kaimuki Writers Workshop regulars. And then for the inspiration of how to take care of family and their exhibition of both grit and inanity throughout, I thank my parents.

ABOUT THE AUTHOR

Virginia Loo has a doctorate in epidemiology, but doesn't practice public health anymore. Except in times of global pandemics, in which case everyone thinks they are an epidemiologist, so she does too. She lives in Honolulu with her family.

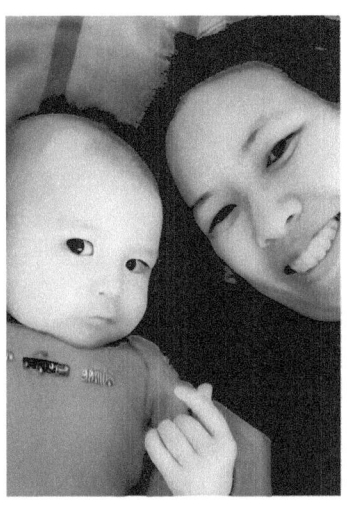

www.ingramcontent.com/pod-product-compliance
Lightning Source LLC
Chambersburg PA
CBHW020228130626

46549CB00005B/1793